• HISTORY OF AFRICA •

HISTORY OF CENTRAL AFRICA

THE DIAGRAM GROUP

Facts On File, Inc.

History of Africa: History of Central Africa
Copyright © 2003 by The Diagram Group

Diagram Visual Information Ltd

Editorial director:	Denis Kennedy
Editor:	Peter Harrison
Contributor:	Ann Kramer
Consultant:	Keith Lye
Indexer:	Martin Hargreaves
Senior designer:	Lee Lawrence
Designers:	Claire Bojczuk
Illustrators:	Kathy McDougall, Graham Rosewarne
Research:	Neil McKenna, Patricia Robertson

Facts On File, Inc.
132 West 31st Street
New York NY 10001

Library of Congress Cataloging-in-Publication Data
History of Central Africa / The Diagram Group.
     p. cm. – (History of Africa)
  Includes bibliographical references and index.
  ISBN 0-8160-5060-0 (set) – ISBN 0-8160-5064-3
  1. Africa, Central–History–Miscellanea. I. Diagram Group. II. Series.

DT352.5 .H59 2003
967–dc21   2002035208

Facts On File books are available at special discounts when purchased in bulk quantities for businesses, associations, institutions, or sales promotions. Please call our Special Sales Department in New York at 212/967-8800 or 800/322-8755.

You can find Facts On File on the World Wide Web at: http://www.factsonfile.com

Printed in the United States of America

EB DIAG 10 9 8 7 6 5 4 3 2 1

Contents

© DIAGRAM

FOREWORD

The six-volume History of Africa series has been designed as a companion set to the Peoples of Africa series. Although, inevitably, there is some overlap between the two series, there is also a significant shift in focus from one to the other. Whereas Peoples of Africa's ethnographic emphasis focuses on the individual human societies which make up the continent, History of Africa graphically presents a historical overview of the political forces that have shaped this vast continent.

History of Central Africa starts off with a description of the region in depth, including its religions, land, climate, and the languages spoken there today, with particular relevance to the colonial legacy as it affected the spoken word region-by-region. There then follows an overview of events from prehistory to the present day, and a brief discussion of the various historical sources, such as travelers' tales, that help us to learn about the past.

The major part of the book comprises an in-depth examination of the history of the region from the first humans through the early civilizations or chiefdoms; the development of trade with other countries; the arrival of European colonists, and the effect this had on the indigenous peoples; the struggles for independence in the last century; and the current political situation in each of the nation, or island, states, in the new millennium.

Interspersed throughout the main text of the book are special features on a variety of political topics or historical themes which bring the region to life, such as Nzinga, the "Warrior Queen," "People of the Throwing Knife," War in the Congo, the Mobutu regime, and Zambia since independence.

Throughout the book the reader will find timelines which list major events; and also maps, diagrams and illustrations, presented in two-color throughout, which help to explain these events in more detail, and place them within the context of world events.

Finally, there is a glossary which defines unfamiliar words used within the book, and a comprehensive index.

Taken together with the other five volumes in this series, *History of Central Africa* will provide the reader with a memorable snapshot of Africa as a continent with a rich history.

Dates

In this book, we use the dating system BCE – Before Common Era – and CE – Common Era. 1 CE is the same year as 1 AD. We have used this system to acknowledge different religions and beliefs, some of which do not recognize the system BC – Before Christ – and AD – *Anno Domini* – which is a Christian dating system.

The religions of Central Africa

The main religious practice in Central Africa is a blend of Christianity and African religion. Christian missionaries visited the region from the 15th century onward, the majority of them during the 19th century. About one percent of the population in Gabon and the Democratic Republic of Congo are Muslim (followers of Islam), rising to eight percent in the Central African Republic.

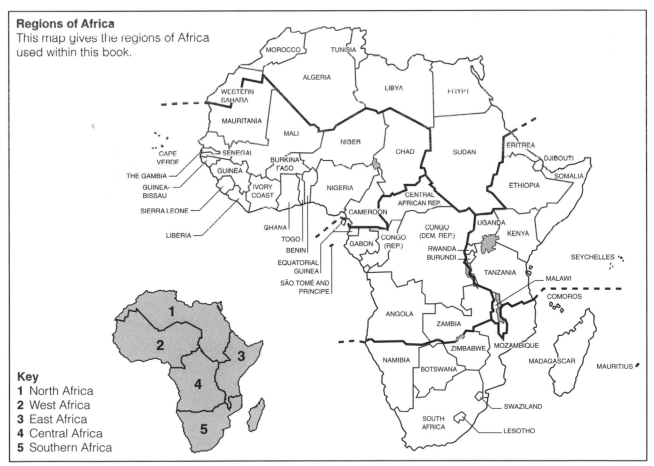

Regions of Africa
This map gives the regions of Africa used within this book.

Key
1 North Africa
2 West Africa
3 East Africa
4 Central Africa
5 Southern Africa

©DIAGRAM

The region

Land

Central Africa consists of eight countries: Angola, Central African Republic, the Democratic Republic of Congo, the Republic of Congo, Equatorial Guinea, Gabon, Zambia, and the island nation of São Tomé and Príncipe. A fertile region, Central Africa is bordered by the Atlantic Ocean to the west, and the highlands and forests of West Africa to the north. Lying to the east is the Great Rift Valley.

Central Africa is divided into three main regions: the huge Congo Basin, which makes up the region's heartland and is drained by the Congo River and its many tributaries; plateaus and mountains, which stretch to the north and south of the Congo Basin, and rise to more than 8,000 ft (2,400 m); and the coastal lowlands, a narrow strip running north to south where Central Africa meets the Atlantic Ocean. Many rivers and lakes drain the region. The Congo River runs 2,716 miles (4,371 m) from south-eastern Congo (Democratic Republic of) to the Atlantic Ocean, and is Africa's longest river after the Nile. The spectacular Victoria Falls lie on the Zambezi River. São Tomé and Príncipe are mountainous volcanic islands covered with tropical forest.

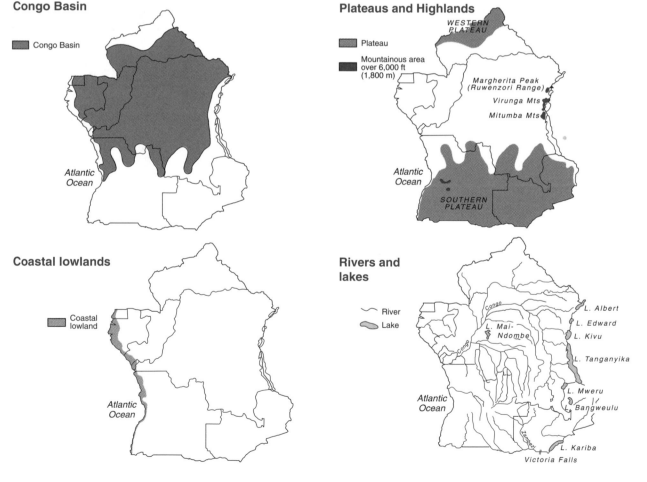

Congo Basin

- Congo Basin

Atlantic Ocean

Plateaus and Highlands

WESTERN PLATEAU

- Plateau
- Mountainous area over 6,000 ft (1,800 m)

Margherita Peak (Ruwenzori Range)
Virunga Mts
Mitumba Mts

Atlantic Ocean

SOUTHERN PLATEAU

Coastal lowlands

- Coastal lowland

Atlantic Ocean

Rivers and lakes

- River
- Lake

Congo
L. Mai-Ndombe
Congo
Atlantic Ocean
Zambezi
Victoria Falls

L. Albert
L. Edward
L. Kivu
L. Tanganyika
L. Mweru
L. Bangweulu
L. Kariba

Climate

Lying within the tropics, Central Africa's climate is always hot or warm. Temperatures near the equator hardly vary; nearer the coast and in the mountains there is a greater swing. Much of the Congo Basin averages a monthly temperature of 21–27 °C (70–80 °F) and in the central Congo Basin the air feels very humid. The region receives plenty of rain. Annual averages range from 180 in (457 cm) on the mountainous coast of Equatorial Guinea to 2 in (5 cm) in southwestern Angola. Northern and southern areas, away from the equator, have tropical climates with distinct wet and dry seasons.

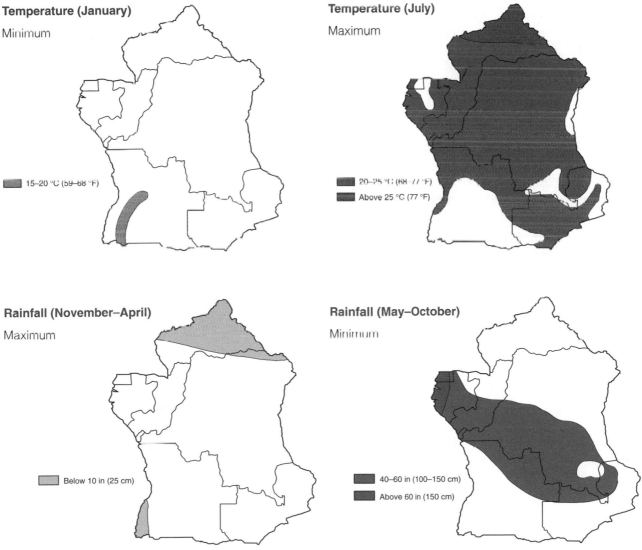

Temperature (January)

Minimum

15–20 °C (59–68 °F)

Temperature (July)

Maximum

20–25 °C (68–77 °F)

Above 25 °C (77 °F)

Rainfall (November–April)

Maximum

Below 10 in (25 cm)

Rainfall (May–October)

Minimum

40–60 in (100–150 cm)

Above 60 in (150 cm)

Central Africa today

Angola
Controlled by Portugal from the 17th century, it achieved independence in 1975. Since then, it has experienced continuous civil war as rival groups – chiefly MPLA, UNITA, and, for a while, the western-backed FNLA – fought for power. Multiparty elections were held in 1992 and a coalition government was formed in 1997. In April 2002 a ceasefire was agreed following the death of UNITA leader, Jonas Savimbi.

Central African Republic (CAR)
Formerly controlled by France, it achieved independence in 1960. In 1962 the country became a one-party state. In 1966 General Bokassa seized power and ruled as a dictator until 1979, when he was overthrown. Since then it has slowly made the transition to democracy. The first multiparty elections took place in 1993. In 2001 an attempted coup was put down with Libyan help.

Congo (Democratic Republic of)
Independent in 1960, it was known as Zaire between 1971–1997. In 1965 the army seized power under General Mobutu, who ruled as a dictator until ousted by Laurent Kabila in 1997. In 1998 civil war broke out when rebel forces sought to overthrow Kabila, who was backed by forces from Angola, Chad, Namibia, and Zimbabwe. In 2001 Kabila was assassinated and, in 2002, peace talks failed to halt the conflict.

Congo (Republic of)
It became independent in 1960, a one-party state in 1964 and, in 1970, adopted communism. In 1990, under Sassou-Nguesso, it abandoned communism and moved towards a market economy. Democracy was restored in 1992 when free elections were held, returning Lissouba as president. Conflict erupted in the 1990s between Lissouba and Sassou-Nguesso's supporters but ended in 1999. In 2002 Sassou-Nguesso was elected president.

Population density:
people per
sq. mile (sq. km)

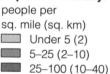

- Under 5 (2)
- 5–25 (2–10)
- 25–100 (10–40)
- 100–500 (40–200)
- Over 500 (200)

Equatorial Guinea
In 1968 it gained independence from Spain. The first president, Francisco Macías Nguema, ruled as a dictator. In 1979 he was overthrown by his nephew, Obiang Nguema. In 1992 a multiparty system was introduced but Nguema's PDGE won elections, despite allegations of electoral irregularities.

Gabon
It achieved independence in 1960. Rich mineral resources have made it the most successful country in Central Africa. From the late 1980s, it moved towards democracy. with opposition parties legalized in 1990.

São Tomé and Príncipe
The islands achieved independence from Portugal in 1975. In 1990 a multiparty constitution was adopted and free elections were held in 1991. In 1995 Príncipe was granted self-government.

Zambia
It became independent as a republic in 1964, with Kaunda as president. In 1972 the country became a one-party state with the United National Independence Party (UNIP) as the only legal party. In 1990 Kaunda legalized opposition parties. The first free elections took place in 1991, when Kaunda was defeated.

Country border
River
Lusaka Capital city

Major city populations
- Over 1,000,000
- 500,000 to 1,000,000
- 300,000 to 500,000
- Under 300,000

CENTRAL
AFRICAN
REPUBLIC

Oubangui

Bangui

EQUATORIAL
GUINEA

Malabo
Bioko Ic.

Bata

Congo

Aruwimi

CONGO
BASIN

Kisangani
Boyoma Falls

Lake
Albert

Lake
Edward

Oubangui

Sanca

São Tomé

Libreville

Ogooué

SÃO TOMÉ
AND
PRÍNCIPE

GABON

CONGO
(REP.)

Congo

Tshuapa

Lomami

Lomela

Lake Kivu

Lake
Mai-Ndombe

Lokoro

Lukenie

CONGO
DEM. REP.

Elila

Brazzaville

Kasai

Sankuru

(Congo-Zaire)

Lualaba

Pointe-Noire

Kinshasa

Kwilu

Lake
Tanganyika

CABINDA
(ANGOLA)

Cabinda

Cuango

Wamba

Loange

Chicapa

Kasai

Lulua

Kananga

Mbuji-Mayi

Luvua

Atlantic
Ocean

Luanda

Cuanza

Lake
Mweru

L. Bangweulu

Luapula

Lubumbashi

Ndola

ANGOLA

Lobito

Huambo

Cassai

Cuito

Cuando

Zambezi

ZAMBIA

Luangwa

Kunene

Lusaka

Kafue

Cubango

Okavango

Kariba Dam
Lake Kariba

Cunene

Victoria Falls

| 0 | 200 | 400 | 600 km |
| 0 | 100 | 200 | 300 | 400 mi |

© DIAGRAM

The languages of Central Africa

Central Africa is home to many ethnic groups, who have emerged as a result of migration, conquest, and intermarriage. Hundreds of languages are spoken, and most of these have regional dialects as well. Each ethnic group has its own language and many groups identify themselves by the language they speak rather than, or as well as, their ethnic origin or nationality. For example, the language of the Azande people, who live in northeast Central African Republic, is Azande (or Pazende). The Bemba language is spoken by the Bemba of

Azande musician
Dressed in an elaborate costume, this man carries a traditional harp-like instrument, which was adorned with a sculpted human-like head.

Zambia, as well as many other people in Zambia and the Democratic Republic of the Congo.

Classifying African languages is a complex undertaking. More than 1,000 languages are spoken across the whole continent. Most are so-called home languages, which are native to the continent. However, many other languages were introduced by European or Asian colonizers or settlers, who arrived on the continent from the 15th century onward. As a result, most Africans speak more than one language – their own ethnic language and a European language. Many also use dialects. The Kongo language has more than fifty dialects. One is called Kileta, a common language used by many Kongo-related people who would otherwise speak different languages from each other.

The colonial legacy

Every country in Central Africa was at some point colonized by Europeans. As a result, European languages are spoken widely and, in some cases, are the official languages of a country. If not the official language, they may used as the language of work and commerce. Portuguese is widely spoken in Angola and São Tomé and Príncipe, English in Zambia, Spanish in Equatorial Guinea, and French in the Central African Republic, Congo, Gabon, and the Democratic Republic of the Congo.

African languages

The home languages used in Central Africa are divided into four main families, within which are several subfamilies. These in turn are divided into groups and subgroups. The languages spoken in Central Africa are printed in italics opposite. (The languages of the Mbuti, Twa, and Mbenga forest peoples are not shown because they tend to speak the same languages as their nearest neighbors.)

African languages

The people of Africa speak more than 1,000 separate languages, most of them "home" languages native to the continent. The remaining languages, such as Arabic, English, or French, have all been introduced by settlers or invaders from Asia or Europe. The home languages are divided into four main families, within which are several subfamilies. These are then divided into groups and again into subgroups. Those languages spoken in Central Africa are printed in *italic* type below.

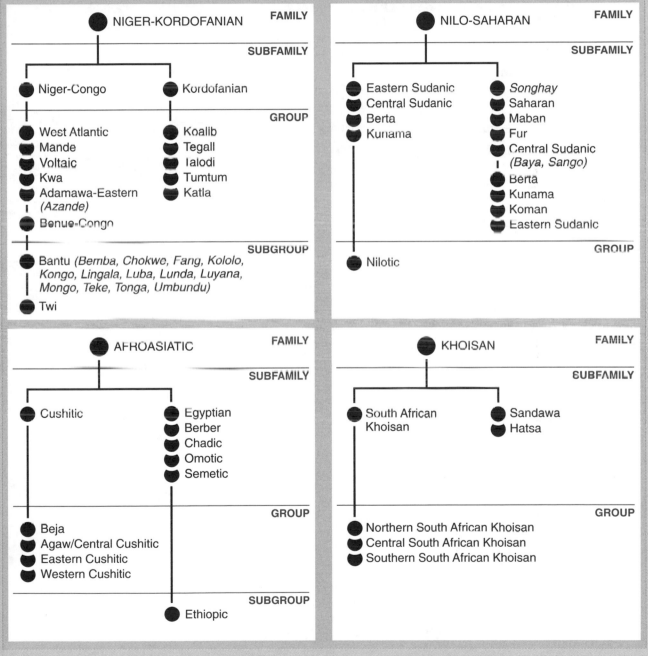

NIGER-KORDOFANIAN — FAMILY

SUBFAMILY
- Niger-Congo
- Kordofanian

GROUP
- West Atlantic
- Mande
- Voltaic
- Kwa
- Adamawa-Eastern *(Azande)*
- Benue-Congo
- Koalib
- Tegali
- Talodi
- Tumtum
- Katla

SUBGROUP
- Bantu *(Bemba, Chokwe, Fang, Kololo, Kongo, Lingala, Luba, Lunda, Luyana, Mongo, Teke, Tonga, Umbundu)*
- Twi

NILO-SAHARAN — FAMILY

SUBFAMILY
- Eastern Sudanic
- Central Sudanic
- Berta
- Kunama
- *Songhay*
- Saharan
- Maban
- Fur
- Central Sudanic *(Baya, Sango)*
- Berta
- Kunama
- Koman
- Eastern Sudanic

GROUP
- Nilotic

AFROASIATIC — FAMILY

SUBFAMILY
- Cushitic
- Egyptian
- Berber
- Chadic
- Omotic
- Semetic

GROUP
- Beja
- Agaw/Central Cushitic
- Eastern Cushitic
- Western Cushitic

SUBGROUP
- Ethiopic

KHOISAN — FAMILY

SUBFAMILY
- South African Khoisan
- Sandawa
- Hatsa

GROUP
- Northern South African Khoisan
- Central South African Khoisan
- Southern South African Khoisan

© DIAGRAM

THE HISTORY

The history of Central Africa dates back thousands of years. The first inhabitants were forest dwellers. Their modern descendants are the Mbuti, Twa, and Mbenga peoples. Most black Central Africans, however, are descended from Bantu-speaking peoples who began arriving in the region in about 100 CE. These people introduced farming and ironworking and gradually displaced or intermarried with earlier inhabitants.

Chiefdoms and states

By the eighth century, more complex societies – states governed by chiefs – were emerging and, by the 12th century, long-distance trade in copper and ivory was established. Over the next 300 years, chiefdoms, kingdoms, and empires were founded throughout Central Africa, including Zambia, the Luba kingdom, and Lunda empire, which dominated the central grasslands of what are now the Democratic Republic of Congo.

Slavery

During the 1400s, Europeans arrived on the west coast and began trading, particularly in African slaves. Slavery was not new to Africa, but the extent of the European slave trade was unprecedented. By the time the trade ended in the 19th century, more than 15 million Africans had been transported across the Atlantic Ocean. The cost in human suffering and disruption to local economies was enormous.

Staff of office
This Luba chief, in contemporary clothes, is holding his traditional staff of office. The geometric patterns are considered to be more important than the human figures, and serve to decorate the staff and, more importantly, to empower the owner.

Colonialism and independence

Initially Europeans confined their influence to the coastal regions but, during the 19th century, explorers and colonizers moved farther inland. Despite resistance from the inhabitants, by the end of the 19th century the whole of Central Africa was under European control.

Colonialism brought some benefits, such as schools and hospitals, but colonial rule, in such places as the Belgian Congo, was often harsh and brutal.

Following World War II (1939–1945), nationalist movements began to emerge and, by 1975, all of what are now the eight countries of Central Africa had achieved independence.

How we know

Information about the history of Central Africa comes from various sources. Archeologists have found early iron tools and excavated sites, such as Ingombe Ilede, an Iron Age trading center, which provide a picture of early lifestyles. Missionaries and explorers produced detailed accounts of their travels and the Africans they encountered, while anthropologists and academics have also added to the evidence.

An act of barbarism
Under Belgian control, African soldiers in the Congo often committed atrocities against their own people.

© DIAGRAM

Historical events

CENTRAL AFRICAN EVENTS	WORLD EVENTS
c.3000 BCE–1000 CE	
c.3000 BCE Ancient Egyptians in contact with rainforest people, Central Africa	**510 BCE** Roman republic founded
c.100 CE Bantu-speaking peoples begin arriving in the region	**c.30 CE** Jesus Christ crucified
c.300 CE Iron-making begins	**622** Muhammad flees to Medina; Islam founded
c.800 Bantu-speaking ironworkers arrive in Congo region	**624** T'ang dynasty unites China
c.850 Chiefs buried with gold at Ingombe Ilede, Zambia	
1001 CE–1500 CE	
c.1200 Bubi people from mainland settle Bioko island (Equatorial Guinea)	**c.1200** Inca Empire founded in the Andes, S. America
1200s Mpongwe people settle what is now Gabon	**1206** Genghis Khan begins Mongol conquest, Asia
c.1300 Kongo kingdom established on Congo River (Angola, Dem. Republic of Congo)	**1346–1349** The Plague (Black Death) sweeps through Europe
1300–1400 Ingombe Ilede is major trading center	**1368** Ming Dynasty, China
1400 Ndongo kingdom established	**1492** Christopher Columbus arrives in the Americas
1482–1483 Portuguese reach coast and encounter Kongo	
1485 Portuguese begin colonizing São Tomé and Príncipe	
1491 Nzinga Kuwu, king of Kongo, converts to Christianity	
1500s Ingombe Ilede abandoned	
1501–1800	
1506 Civil war begins in Kongo kingdom	**1519–1522** Ferdinand Magellan sails around the world
1520s Kongo supply slaves to Portuguese colony, Sâo Tomé	**1521** Spain conquers Aztecs
1548 Jesuit missionaries arrive in Kongo	**1526** Mughal Empire founded, India
1550 Lunda Kingdom emerges (Dem. Rep. of Congo)	**1590s** Dutch arrive at the Cape (South Africa)
1556 War between Kongo and Ndongo	**1619** First African slaves arrive in Jamestown, Virginia, US
1560–1880 Slave trade flourishes on Central African coast	**c.1760** Industrial Revolution begins in Britain
1568 Jaga invade Kongo	**1776–1783** American Revolution
1576 Portuguese establish slave depot at Luanda (Angola)	**1789–1799** French Revolution
1619 Portuguese and Jaga conquer Ndongo Kingdom	
1623 Nzinga Nbandi becomes queen of Ndongo and fights Portuguese	
1641 Dutch take Luanda from Portuguese	
c.1650 Bemba kingdom founded (Zambia)	
1665–1670 Portuguese establish rule over Kongo	
1700s Lozi kingdom (Zambia) and Lunda Empire (Dem. Rep. of Congo) exist; Kuba kingdoms develop in central Congo region	
1777 Portuguese claim what is now Equatorial Guinea	
1800 Kazambe (Zambia) controls trade routes across the continent; Fang begin to settle (Gabon)	
1801–1850	
1805–1830 Baya settle what is now Central African Republic	**1804** Napoleon becomes emperor of France
1830s Lunda Empire ends	**1821–1830** Greek War of Independence
1835 Nguni, fleeing Zulu expansion, settle what is now Zambia	**1848** Marx and Engels publish *The Communist Manifesto*
1843–1858 Spain sets up Spanish Guinea (Equatorial Guinea)	

CENTRAL AFRICAN EVENTS	WORLD EVENTS
1851–1900	
1852–1873 David Livingstone explores Central Africa, opening the region to colonization	**1861** Italy is unified
1858 Portuguese abolish slavery	**1868** Meiji restoration, Japan
1885 Belgian King Léopold II creates personal colony: Congo Free State (Dem. Rep. of Congo)	**1869** Suez Canal opens
	1871 Unification of Germany
1889 French establish outpost at Bangui (Central African Republic)	**1884** Berlin Conference on Africa
1890 British South Africa Company (BSAC) takes over Lozi kingdom as Barotseland	**1898** Spanish-American War
1891 French create colony of French Congo	**1899–1902** Anglo-Boer War
1897–1900 BSAC conquer Bemba, who become part of Northern Rhodesia (Zambia)	
1899 British conquer Kazembe	
1901–1950	
1902–1903 Balinda War against Portuguese colonization (Angola)	**1904–1905** Russo-Japanese War
1908 Belgian government takes over Congo Free State and renames it Belgian Congo	**1905** First Russian Revolution
	1914–1918 World War I
1910 Gabon becomes part of French Equatorial Africa	**1917** Russian Revolution: Bolsheviks take power
1920s–1930s Copper mining developed in Northern Rhodesia (Zambia)	**1929** Wall Street Crash, US, leads to worldwide economic depression
1921–1935 Up to 20,000 Africans die building the Congo-Atlantic Ocean railway (Dem. Rep. of Congo)	
1923–1924 British government takes control of Northern Rhodesia (Zambia) and Southern Rhodesia (Zimbabwe). Africans forced into reserves. White settlers encouraged.	**1939–1945** World War II
	1946 United Nations formed
	1948 Apartheid introduced, South Africa
1946 Nationalist movement (Federation of Welfare Societies) emerges in Northern Rhodesia (Zambia)	**1949** North Atlantic Treaty Organization (NATO) formed
1949 Independence movement forms (Central African Republic)	**1950–1953** Korean War
1951–1970	
1950s Kariba Dam built on Zambezi River	**1955** Warsaw Pact formed, eastern Europe
1953 Northern Rhodesia (Zambia), Southern Rhodesia(Zimbabwe), and Nyasaland (Malawi) merged into white-minority ruled Central African Federation (CAF)	**1959** Fidel Castro leads Cuban revolution
	1962 Cuban missile crisis
1956 Popular Movement for Liberation of Angola (MPLA) formed	**1963** US president John F. Kennedy assassinated
1957 Oil discoveries made in Congo region	**1965–1973** US troops fight in Vietnam
1958 Zambia Africa National Congress (ZANC) set up with Kenneth Kaunda as president	**1967** Six-Day War between Israel and Egypt and other Arab nations
1960 South Kasai and Katanga provinces announce secession leading to civil war (Dem. Rep. of Congo)	**1967–1970** Biafran Civil War, Nigeria
1960 CAR, Dem. Rep. of Congo, and Gabon gain independence	**1969** Neil Armstrong lands on the Moon
1960–1963 Katanga secession causes civil war (Dem. Rep. of Congo)	
1961 Angolan War of Independence begins	

Colonial occupation and independence

CENTRAL AFRICAN EVENTS	WORLD EVENTS
1962 Central African Republic becomes one party state	
1962 Northern Angolan rebels form Front for Liberation of Angola (FNLA)	
1963 One-party state set up in Republic of Congo	
1963 Dem. Rep. of Congo reunited	
1963 CAF dissolved	
1964 Military coup, Gabon; French reinstall Leon M'Ba	
1964 Northern Rhodesia independent as Zambia; Kenneth Kaunda is president	
1965 Mobutu Sese Seko takes power in Dem. Rep. of Congo, bans political parties.	
1965 Military coup, Central African Republic; Jean-Bédel Bokassa takes power	
1966 Southern Angolan rebels form National Union for Total Liberation of Angola (UNITA)	
1968 Gabon becomes a one-party state	
1968 Macias Nguema elected president, Equatorial Guinea	
1970–1979 Macias sets up a one-party state in Equatorial Guinea, and conducts reign of terror	

1971–1980

CENTRAL AFRICAN EVENTS	WORLD EVENTS
1971 Mobutu aims to reduce foreign influence; renames Dem. Rep. of Congo as Zaire	**1973** Arabs ban oil sales to US; sets off worldwide oil crisis
1972 Zambia becomes one-party state	**1973** Yom Kippur War between Egypt and Israel
1972 Bokassa declares himself "president for life," in Central African "Empire"	**1979** Islamic fundamentalists seize power in Iran
1975 Civil begins in Angola between Soviet-and Cuban-backed MPLA, South African-and US-backed UNITA, and FNLA; MPLA form government	**1979** Soviet Union invades Afghanistan
1975 São Tomé and Príncipe becomes independent	**1980–1988** Iran-Iraq War
1976 Bokassa names himself "emperor" of Central African "Empire"	
1976 Second Shaba War, unsucessful Katangan rebellion	
1977 Martial law declared in Congo	
1977 First Shaba War, Zaire (Dem. Rep. of Congo)	
1979 Bokassa ousted, Central African "Empire"	
1979 Military coup ousts Macías Nguema, Equatorial Guinea	

1981–2002

CENTRAL AFRICAN EVENTS	WORLD EVENTS
1985 Equatorial Guinea adopts African Franc Zone currency	**1982–1985** Israel invades Lebanon
1988 South African and Cuban forces begin withdrawal from Angola	**1989** Revolution in Romania
1990 One-party rule ends in Gabon with elections	**1990** East and West Germany reunited
1990 Mobutu announces plans to make Zaire a multiparty democracy (Dem. Rep. of Congo)	**1990–1991** Gulf War follows Iraqi invasion of Kuwait
1991 Opposition parties legalized in Congo and CAR	**1991** Communism collapses in USSR and eastern Europe
1991 Multiparty elections held in Zambia and São Tomé and Príncipe	**1991** Apartheid ends, South Africa
1991 Multiparty constitution drafted in Zaire but transition to democracy frustrated and rioting breaks out	

CENTRAL AFRICAN EVENTS

1992 MPLA wins elections in Angola. UNITA does not accept results and civil war begins
1992 Multiparty constitutions agreed: Republic of Congo and Equatorial Guinea
1993 UN imposes sanctions against UNITA
1993 Multiparty elections held in CAR
1994 MPLA and UNITA sign peace treaty; conflict continues
1994 Economic hardship and social unrest in Congo, Equatorial Africa, Gabon, and CAR
1994 More than 2 million refugees enter Zaïre (Dem. Rep. of Congo)
1995 Commission reports human rights abuses in Zambia
1995 UN peacekeeping force arrives in Angola
1996 Angola and São Tomé and Príncipe join Community of Portuguese-speaking countries
1996 Rwandan-backed Zairean Tutsi take up arms against government (Dem. Rep. of Congo)
1998 Civil war breaks out in Dem. Rep. of Congo
1999 Civil war continues, Angola
1999 Obiang Nguema elected president, Equatorial Guinea amid allegations of vote rigging
2001 Libya helps to put down attempted coup in CAR
2001–2002 Outbreak of Ebola virus, Gabon
2002 Ceasefire agreed, Angola
2002 Peace talks fail to halt civil war, Dem. Rep. of Congo

WORLD EVENTS

1992 Cold War ends
1994–1996 Civil war, Rwanda; conflict spreads to Burundi
1998 Good Friday Agreement, peace in Northern Ireland
2001 Terrorist attack on World Trade Center, New York
2002 Israeli-Arab conflict

COLONIAL OCCUPATION AND INDEPENDENCE

Country	Independence	Occupied*	Colonial power
Angola	Nov 11, 1975	1670	Portugal
Central African Republic (as Oubangui-Chari, part of French Equatorial Africa)	Aug 13, 1960	1894	France
Congo (as Middle, or French, Congo, part of French Equatorial Africa)	Aug 15, 1960	1885	France
Equatorial Guinea Bioko Island (as Fernando Póo)	Oct 12, 1968	1845 (mainland) 1493 1778	Spain Portugal Spain
Gabon (as part of French Equatorial Africa)	Aug 17, 1960	1839	France
São Tomé and Príncipe	July 12, 1975	1493	Portugal
Dem. Rep. of Congo (as the Congo Free State and then as the Belgian Congo)	June 30, 1960	1876	Belgium
Zambia (as Northern Rhodesia)	Oct 24, 1964	1890	Britain

* The years given for the beginning of colonial occupation of the modern-day nation states are those by which a significant area of coastal and hinterland territory had been effectively occupied by a colonial power.

© DIAGRAM

EARLY PEOPLES

Archeologists have not found hominid remains in Central Africa and our knowledge about the origins of the very earliest peoples is limited. The first inhabitants were probably forest-dwelling peoples, who lived in the dense tropical rainforests of what is now the Congo region, or sometimes on the grasslands. The Ancient Egyptians, from the northern part of the continent, knew about these early inhabitants some 5,000 years ago.

The early forest dwellers were hunter-gatherers who were highly skilled in forest lore. They hunted game, and gathered forest products, such as fruit, nuts, and wild honey. They used wooden or stone tools and cooked their meat over fires. They lived in isolated communities, clearing an area in the forest where they set up small, conical huts for shelters. Their descendants today are the Mbuti, Twa, and Mbenda peoples, sometimes insultingly known as pygmies, because of their short stature.

Bantu arrivals

From about the 100s CE, new people began arriving in
Central Africa. They were Bantu speakers, who probably
originated in an area between what are now Cameroon
and Nigeria more than 2,000 years ago, and traveled
eastward in East Africa and southward into Central and
Southern Africa. They did not all arrive at once but
traveled into the region in waves of migration over
several hundred years. In Zambia, there is evidence of at
least three migration routes: from the great lakes, from the
Congo forest, and from what is now Angola.

By about the 800s CE, Bantu speakers had reached what
is now the Democratic Republic of the Congo and, by
about 1000 CE, they were settled in northern Zambia.
Dispersing through the region, they absorbed existing
hunter-gatherers into their communities, or displaced
them. Today, most of Central Africa's population is
descended from those early Bantu-speaking settlers.

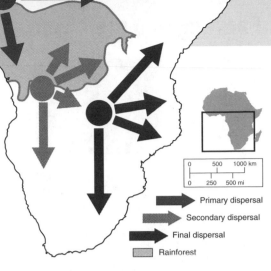

Primary dispersal	
Secondary dispersal	
Final dispersal	
Rainforest	

Bantu languages (above)

This map shows the probable dispersal of
the Bantu languages during the period
100 BCE to 600 CE on the African continent.

Forest home (below)

Temporary shelters had a frame made from
saplings which was then covered in leaves
and ferns to provide a canopy. Camps
moved on and reorganized elsewhere in
order not to empty one area of game.

Farming and metalworking

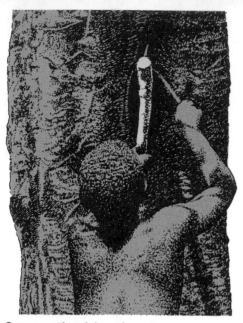

Conservation (above)
Some Central African countries are now applying the knowledge of forest-dwelling people to help conserve their national parks.

Mongo craftsmanship (below)
The necklace (below left) was made by Mongo artisans skilled in making iron jewelry, whereas the wooden-handled knife (below right) is a fine example of their skill in making weapons from iron.

The Bantu-speaking peoples who arrived in Central Africa were farmers, who introduced pastoralism or cattle breeding into the region, together with crop cultivation and farming tools, such as the hoe. Over time, crops included millet, which grew particularly well in the tropics, oil palm, and bananas.

They dug pits for furnaces, which they surrounded with bellows, and produced iron tools and weapons. These were used not only locally but also for trade, which began to develop gradually. Archeologists have also found evidence of pottery technology which suggest that the Iron-Age farmers were skilled pot makers who decorated their pots with grooves and patterns.

By the end of the first millennium CE, Bantu-speaking people were also working copper, particularly in the mines of the Katanga region of what is now the Democratic Republic of the Congo. Workers there cast copper ingots into molds to produce goods for personal use and for trade. Copper was used for jewelry, rings, bangles, chains, necklaces and ornaments, and to decorate spearshafts and shields. The Katanga mines were to remain a major copper-producing source for the next 1,000 years.

Communities and chiefs

The Bantu adapted successfully to their new environment. Wherever they settled, they established village communities. They also developed a system of statehood.

Some historians believe that the idea of using chiefs, whether headmen or kings, to govern or rule communities began in the Congo grasslands, around the Katanga lakes, in about the eighth century. From these beginnings, more

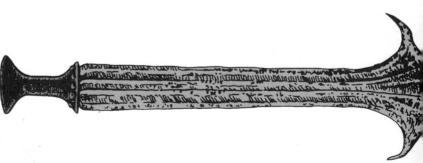

complex and larger political groupings or states began to emerge throughout Central Africa, some of which were established by the 13th century.

Using the river systems of the Congo basins, these early chiefs were able to develop trading and cultural links over wide areas.

Trade

Archeological evidence shows that villages were trading with each other as early as the fifth century CE. Bangles or cowrie shells have been found in areas where there was no copper. From the ninth century, however, long-distance trade in iron, copper, cattle, and ivory was becoming established. It was mainly based on Iron-Age centers, such as Ingombe Ilede in what is now Zambia.

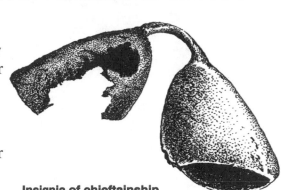

Insignia of chieftainship
Double iron gongs were just one of the emblems associated with the office of chieftain among the people of the Congo forests in Central Africa.

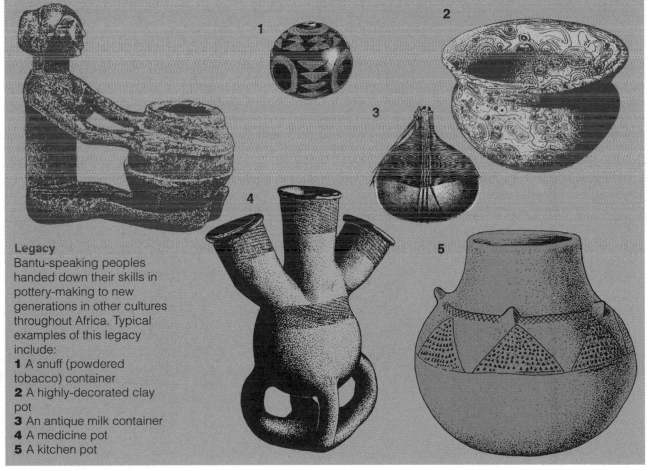

Legacy
Bantu-speaking peoples handed down their skills in pottery-making to new generations in other cultures throughout Africa. Typical examples of this legacy include:
1 A snuff (powdered tobacco) container
2 A highly-decorated clay pot
3 An antique milk container
4 A medicine pot
5 A kitchen pot

© DIAGRAM

Ingombe Ilede

Archeologists have uncovered the remains of an important farming community and burial site near the area where the Zambezi and Kafue rivers meet in what is now Zambia. The site is called Ingombe Ilede, which literally means "where the cow sleeps." Graves uncovered by the archeologists date back to the 15th century and contain the skeletal remains of local rulers, which are adorned with necklaces of local gold and imported glass beads, and the remains of fine cloth burial shrouds.

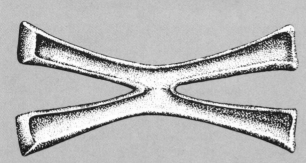

Copper ingot (above)
This X-shaped metal bar, which is over 1 ft (30 cm) in length, came from Ingombe Ilede, and was used as a form of local currency at the time.

Traditional architecture (below)
These are three examples of structures built in the traditional style:
1 a peanut store;
2 a stilt-house, comprising a ring of poles to support the roof, walls made of sticks plastered with mud, and a platform in the center;
3 a mud and grass grain store. Nowadays, modern building materials, such as brick and cement, are becoming much more popular.

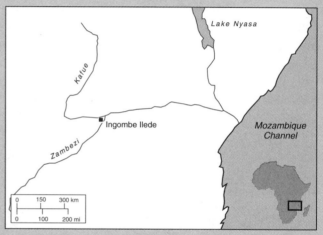

Local trade center and market for foreign trade
Ingombe Ilede played an important part in transcontinental trade. It had links with both Great Zimbabwe (situated in present-day Zimbabwe) and the trading cities on the east coast of Africa.

Ingombe Ilede was an important center of wealth and trade. It may have been occupied as early as the seventh century and reached its greatest extent in the 15th century. It was a time of increasing trade, which encouraged local clans to group together under the rule of a single chief. The chief's court served as a center for transcontinental trade. Foodstuffs, iron, copper, salt, cotton, cloth, tobacco, baskets, and pottery were among the items traded.

Ingombe Ilede is the best documented and one of the most famous Iron-Age centers in Zambia. It would have traded locally, but its inhabitants were also involved in long-distance trade with people farther south, in Great Zimbabwe, exporting gold down the Zambezi via traders coming from the Indian Ocean, and with trading cities on the east coast. Copper crosses have also been found at the site – probably a form of currency used with local merchants and traders from outside the region.

By 1400 non-African, mainly Muslim, traders were venturing farther inland, following trade routes that were already well established, and they would have traded with Ingombe Ilede. However, although what is now known as Zambia continued to trade with non-Africans, Ingombe Ilede itself was abandoned during the 1500s.

Secrets of the past

This skeleton was buried with hammerheads, copper wire, and iron tongs. Shells from the East African coast encircle the neck, and bangles adorn the limbs.

COASTAL KINGDOMS

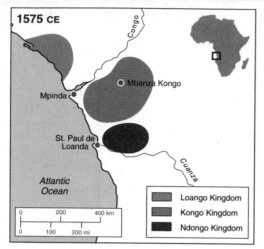

Three kingdoms
This map shows the location of Loango, Kongo and Ndongo on the western coast of Central Africa in 1573 CE.

From the 14th century, a series of centralized kingdoms developed on the western coast of Central Africa. The most powerful was the Kongo kingdom, which at its height extended from what are now the southern part of the Congo Republic and the western area of the Democratic Republic of the Congo as far as northern Angola. Farther inland, and to the south of the Kongo kingdom, was the Ndongo kingdom. Founded in the 15th century, for many years it paid tribute to the Kongo. To the north was the Loango state.

Both the Kongo and Ndongo kingdoms had emerged from smaller Bantu-speaking metalworking and cattle-owning communities, which had become wealthy from long-distance trade in salt, iron, ivory and other goods. They also captured slaves from the interior.

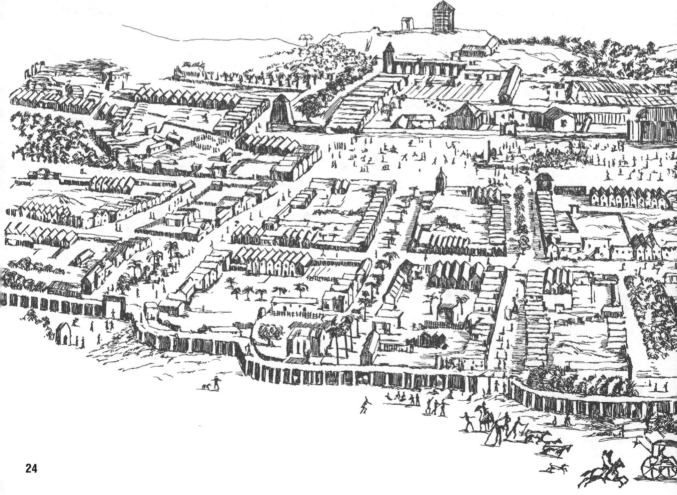

In the late 15th century, Portuguese explorers and traders arrived on the west coast as part of their search for a route around Africa to Asia. They introduced Christianity – particularly Roman Catholicism – into the region and established trading relationships with the Kongo. Subsequently, they moved south and traded with the Ndongo kingdom.

Increasingly, the slave trade became the leading economic activity in the region and relationships between the Kongo, Ndongo, and Portuguese soured, leading to conflict. Ultimately, the slave trade destroyed the economic and political stability of the two kingdoms. By the late 17th century, the Kongo kingdom had fragmented and Ndongo lands had come under Portuguese control.

Growth and decline of the kingdoms	
1300s	Kongo kingdom founded on Congo River
1300s–1400s	Ingombe Ilede trades with east coast
1400s	Ndongo kingdom established south of Kongo
1470s	Portuguese discover islands of São Tomé and Príncipe and settle colony there; it becomes base for slave trading
1482–1483	Portuguese reach Angolan coast and mouth of Congo River
1490	Nzinga Nkuwu, king of Kongo, converts to Christianity
1494	Factions develop in Kongo kingdom for, and against, the Portuguese
1556	Ndongo kingdom breaks away from Kongo kingdom
1568	Jaga from interior invade Kongo kingdom
1665	Battle of Mbwila (Ambuila): Portuguese defeat Kongo armies; Kongo kingdom fragments
1671	Portuguese gain control of Ndongo lands

The state of Loango
This illustration, based on a 17th-century engraving of Loango, shows the royal palaces and gardens in the background. A level of sophistication, culture and material success is evident in its construction, an effect of the long-distance trade in salt, iron, and ivory giving way to the more profitable slave trade.

©DIAGRAM

Kongo kingdom

The Kongo kingdom evolved in the late 14th century when a group of Bakongo (Kongo) people moved south of the Congo River into what is now northern Angola. Under the first known king, known as Nimi, who had married the daughter of a Kongo chief, they conquered the people they found there and established a capital at Mbanza. By the middle of the 15th century, the Kongo kingdom was the most powerful state on the western coast of Central Africa.

Kongo rulers were known as *manikongo*. The *manikongo* was the ruler, military leader, and spiritual head of the kingdom. Assisted by a council of ministers, he ruled over a large territory and received tributes from many people, including the Ndongo kingdom. Taxes were collected and there was an official currency based on shells. Wealth came from long-distance trade in items, such as ivory and copper, and the kingdom expanded through trade alliances and marriages.

Antonio Nigrita (above)
He was the ambassador of the Kongo kingdom to the Vatican State, and he died in 1608. This illustration is based on a bust of Nigrita which was sculpted by Francesco Caporale.

In 1482 the Portuguese explorer Diogo Cão reached the mouth of the Congo River and made contact with the Kongo, the first kingdom on the west coast of Central Africa to encounter Europeans. The Kongo king and ruling class welcomed the chance to

A royal welcome
In this illustration King Alvaro II of Kongo is shown welcoming ambassadors from Holland to his court. Dutch and Portuguese colonial powers were rivals for control of the various kingdoms situated near the mouth of the Congo river at the end of the sixteenth century.

trade with the Portuguese and the two kingdoms –
Portugal and Kongo – exchanged emissaries. For the
Portuguese, the Kongo meant riches for the Portuguese
crown but the *manikongo* was also a leader to be
respected. They formed an alliance whereby the
Portuguese provided technical and military advice in
exchange for trading rights, particularly in such goods as
ivory and gold, and also in slaves.

The Portuguese king, Joao II and the *manikongo*,
Nzinga a Nkuwu, also formed an alliance. Nkuwu
converted to Christianity and was baptized Joao I, like his
Portuguese counterpart. His son, Nzinga Mbemba, a
devout Christian, was baptized Afonso, later Afonso I.
Four young Bakongo men were sent to Portugal to be
educated and the Portuguese gave the Kongo carpenters,
masons, horses and cattle, and a printing press.

Afonso I, who ruled the Kongo from 1506–1543
initially continued the alliance with Portugal,
participating in the slave trade for the sake of revenue.
But Portugal began to lose interest in the kingdom, seeing
it only as a source of slaves. As missionaries left and
more slave traders arrived, relations between the two
powers deteriorated. The Portuguese encouraged internal
rebellion and by the 1520s the kingdom was in turmoil,
the authority of the *manikongo* had been undermined, and
the Portuguese had effectively taken control.

In 1568 the Jaga (also Imbangala), Lunda people from
northeast Angola, invaded the kingdom. They were
repulsed with Portuguese help and some stability
returned. The Kongo king tried to break free from
Portuguese influence by making overtures to the Dutch,
but in 1665 the Portuguese defeated Kongo armies,
and the kingdom collapsed.

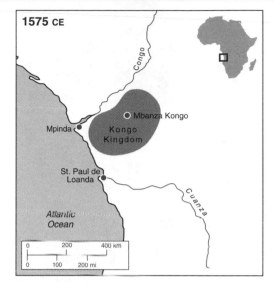

Kongo kingdom
This map shows the extent
of the kingdom in 1575,
shortly after it had been
under threat from the Jaga.

Capital city
This illustration is based on a 16th-
century engraving of Mbanza, the
capital of the Kongo kingdom from
the 14th century until its
destruction by the Jaga people in
the latter part of the 16th century.

©DIAGRAM

27

Ndongo kingdom

The Ndongo kingdom lay inland and south of the Kongo. It was founded by Mbundu farmers in the second half of the 15th century and ruled by leaders known as *ngola*, who were subservient to the Kongo kings and paid them tribute. The Portuguese, who called the Ndongo kingdom the kingdom of Benguela, changed the pronunciation of *ngola* to "Angola" and subsequently used this name to refer to the whole area.

For many years the Portuguese ignored the Ndongo kingdom, concentrating on trading with the Kongo. However, they arrived in the region in the mid-16th century and, by the 1540s, the Ndongo kingdom, which controlled the region's trade in salt and iron, was providing slaves for Portuguese traders from São Tomé, where there were plantations.

Angered by this, and keen to maintain a monopoly on the trade, the Kongo king went to war against the Ndongo. The *ngola*'s army routed the Kongo and, in 1556, broke away from the Kongo kingdom, making Ndongo independent. This left the *ngolo* in control of a large territory between the Lukela and Cuanza rivers.

Francisco d'Almeida
The first Governor-General of Angola who, in 1592, disputed land ownership with earlier settlers. An open revolt ensued, as a result of which he was expelled from the colony.

The Portuguese in Angola
In 1575 the Portuguese founded the coastal city of Luanda, which was situated west of Ndongo, as a base for the slave trade. Part of the legacy left by the Portuguese was a number of Roman Catholic churches, one of which is shown here.

The *ngola* asked Portugal for military support and an expedition was sent from Lisbon, after which the Portuguese tried to colonize the area. Keen to expand their slave trading, and beset with problems in the Kongo kingdom, in 1575 the Portuguese founded the coastal city of Luanda, west of Ndongo, as a base for the slave trade.

They were also attracted by rumors of gold and silver deposits inland and intensified their activities in the Ndongo kingdom, causing resentment. Portuguese settlers and troops arrived in the region and guerrilla warfare broke out between Portugal and the Ndongo kingdom. Tropical diseases and fierce resistance from the Africans slowed the invasion in the 1580s.

Luanda became a Portuguese colony. The Portuguese established forts along the coast and pushed farther into Ndongo territory. The kingdom fiercely resisted the incursion until 1619 when Portuguese forces overthrew Kabesa, the Ndongo capital, and the *ngola* fled the region. The *ngola*'s sister, Queen Nzinga, led resistance against the Portuguese but, by the late 17th century, the entire Ndongo kingdom had been incorporated into Portuguese-controlled Angola.

Ndongo kingdom
This map shows the extent of the kingdom in 1575. From the 15th to the 17th centuries, Portuguese influence grew in the region.

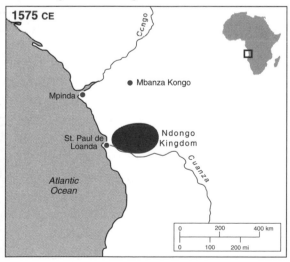

Tomb sculpture
Such sculptures date from the 1800s, but *tumbas*, as they were called, were produced as early as the 1500s in northern Angola, formerly the Ndongo kingdom, before colonization by the Portuguese in the middle of the 16th century.

This example represents a chief chewing a plant stem which he would subsequently have spat out onto lesser members of his tribe during the course of certain rituals.

Nzinga, the "Warrior Queen"

Lateral thinking (right)
Queen Nzinga of Ndongo is shown negotiating with the Portuguese colonial authorities. As they neglected on this occasion to provide a seat for her, she used one of her unfortunate servants as a chair.

Noblemen (below)
These Kongo noblemen, from the northern Kingdom of Loango, exacted tribute on a regular basis from the occupants of the southern Kingdom of Ndongo.

From the 1620s until her death in 1663, a remarkable woman led a fierce resistance against the Portuguese. She was Queen Nzinga of the Ndongo.

In 1619 the Portuguese, who were attempting to colonize the Ndongo kingdom, seized the capital Kabasa. The ngola, or ruler, fled the kingdom. His sister, Anna Nzinga, became ruler in his stead.

Queen Nzinga was determined to prevent the Portuguese conquest. Initially she negotiated a treaty with the Portuguese. Her meeting with the Portuguese governor is legendary. She arrived at Luanda in royal splendor but, on entering the room, realized there was no chair for her. She promptly summoned one of her servants, who fell on her hands and knees to provide a seat for the queen. A treaty was signed but the Portuguese, greedy for slaves, did not keep to its terms.

In 1624 Queen Nzinga began a campaign of resistance against the Portuguese. She built up an army from slaves who had fled the Portuguese, called

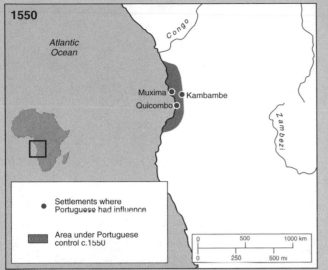

1550

Atlantic Ocean

Congo

Zambezi

Muxima
Kambambe
Quicombo

• Settlements where Portuguese had influence

Area under Portuguese control c.1550

0   500   1000 km
0   250   500 mi

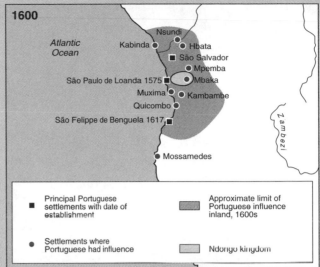

1600

Nsundi

Atlantic Ocean

Kabinda   Hbata
São Salvador
Mpemba
São Paulo de Loanda 1575   Mbaka
Muxima   Kambambe
Quicombo
São Felippe de Benguela 1617

• Mossamedes

Zambezi

■ Principal Portuguese settlements with date of establishment

Approximate limit of Portuguese influence inland, 1600s

• Settlements where Portuguese had influence

Ndongo kingdom

Increasing influence

Portuguese involvement grew in Central Africa, particularly from the fifteenth to the seventeenth centuries. The map (above left) reflects the situation in 1550, and the one (above right) the state of play in 1600.

on Africans under Portuguese rule to rebel, and made an alliance with the Jaga. Nzinga was driven from Ndongo and forced to flee to the north, where she created a land for her people by conquering the kingdom of Matamba.

From Matamba, Queen Nzinga continued to wage war against the Portuguese. A brilliant strategist, she formed an alliance with the Dutch who provided her with a militia of soldiers. Thousands of slave soldiers flocked to her and, although the alliance with the Dutch came to an end, she continued to wage a guerrilla war against the Portuguese. Although aged over 60, she still led her warriors herself.

Finally, however, Queen Nzinga signed a treaty with the Portuguese and most of the Ndongo land was ceded to the ngola, a puppet ruler installed by the Portuguese. Her Matamba kingdom remained independent until her death in 1663.

Ready for battle

This Portuguese soldier, armed with pike and sword, is typical of those opposing Queen Nzinga in Ndongo in the 16th century.

© DIAGRAM

31

The arrival of Christianity

Portuguese traders who arrived on the west coast of Central Africa in the early 1480s were soon followed by Roman Catholic missionaries, particularly Jesuits. Some Central Africans, particularly the Kongo rulers, welcomed them.

One Kongo ruler, Nzinga Nkuwu, later Afonso I, had become fascinated by Christian values early in his life. When young, he had 10 years of clerical instruction and became a devout Christian. He converted to Roman Catholicism and made it the official religion of his kingdom, establishing contact with the Vatican, building churches in the kingdom, and supplying his subjects with images of saints and crucifixes. Afonso requested and welcomed increasing numbers of missionaries and priests, who established mission schools in the region. Afonso's son became a bishop although his nephew, Diogo, who succeeded him, was anti-Roman Catholic and attempted to reverse the Christian influence.

Jesuits also made their way to Luanda and the Ndongo kingdom where, as in the Kongo kingdom, they established churches and mission schools, including a Jesuit college in São Salvador. The Jesuits saw the Africans as souls to be saved and were responsible for education, training some Africans and mixed-race people for the clergy, and administrative positions. The Jesuits also sanctioned, and participated in, the slave trade. They argued that by selling Africans into slavery they would come into contact with Christianity in the American colonies and be converted. Slaves were often baptized before being shipped to the Americas.

Following conflict in the Kongo and Ndongo kingdoms, many Portuguese missionaries left Africa, although their influence remained.

Spreading the word of God

These four maps show the locations of Christian missions, both Roman Catholic and Protestant, in the region of Central Africa at the following times: pre-1800; 1800–1860; 1861–1880; and 1881–1914.

0 500 1000 km
0 250 500 mi

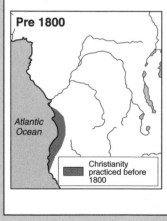

Pre 1800

Atlantic Ocean

Christianity practiced before 1800

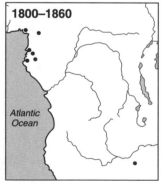

1800–1860

Atlantic Ocean

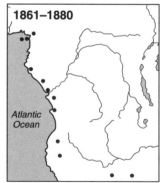

1861–1880

Atlantic Ocean

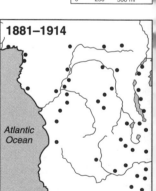

1881–1914

Atlantic Ocean

During the 19th century, European missionaries again arrived in Africa, although this time they moved much farther inland as part of the move to open up the interior of Central Africa to European colonization. Some, such as David Livingstone, were both explorers and missionaries. By the time of their arrival, the slave trade was over and European missionaries concentrated on education and conversion. Many also worked in schools and hospitals.

Kongolese crucifix (left)
This 200 year-old crucifix is typical of those made in the Kongo Kingdom, and used to advance the spread of Christianity in Central Africa in the 1800s.

The Agony in the Garden
This illustration shows a 17th-century brass casting from Angola. It depicts Jesus Christ, the Son of God, in the Garden of Gethsemane. Shadowed by the cross, Jesus prays to his Father in heaven for strength to enable Him to complete His mission.

© DIAGRAM

33

SLAVERY

Man's inhumanity to man
This collar was specifically designed to prevent captured slaves from escaping; it also had the secondary effect of preventing the slaves from lying down to sleep.

Tippu Tib
He was a slave trader who was born in Zanzibar, probably of mixed Arabic and African parentage. His empire was at its height at the start of the 1870s. Slaves originating in Central Africa were exported from either East or West Africa across the Atlantic to the Americas.

The Portuguese arrived on the western coast of Central Africa in the early 1480s. Soon afterwards they began trading with the Kongo Kingdom. One of their main aims was to acquire slaves to work in their colony in Brazil. Other European traders followed and, by the late 16th and early 17th centuries, forts and trading posts had been set up along the coast of West Africa from what is now Senegal to Angola. From this point the trade in African slaves grew enormously as Europeans bought slaves to work the mines and plantations of their colonies in the Americas, and for use as domestic servants. It has been estimated that by the time the trade finally halted in the late 19th century, more than 15 million Africans – men, women, and children – had been sold into slavery and transported across the Atlantic.

A new type of slavery

Slavery had existed both in Africa and elsewhere before the 16th century. The Ancient Egyptians, Greeks, and Romans all used slaves. Later, warring North African Muslims and Christian Spanish and Portuguese often enslaved prisoners of war. Within Africa itself, criminals, debtors, and prisoners of war were commonly enslaved.

However, the type of slavery and the trade in slaves that developed from the 16th century in Africa were unprecedented. Slavery had never been practiced on such a large scale before, nor had it been so closely allied to economic gain. It was one of the largest forced migrations of humans in history, causing terrible human suffering and having a devastating effect on both local communities and economies in Africa.

The development of slavery in Africa

1300s	Kongo Kingdom founded
1400s	Ndongo Kingdom established
1470s	Portuguese discover islands of São Tomé and Príncipe; they become a base for slave trading
1482	Portuguese make contact with Kongo Kingdom
1517	Spain begins shipping Africans to the Americas
1540s	Ndongo supplies slaves to Portuguese
1575	Portuguese found Loanda (Luanda) as a base for slave trade (Angola)
1592	English begin involvement in transatlantic slave trade
1605	Dutch begin to ship African slaves to the Caribbean
1619	First African slaves arrive in Jamestown, Virginia
1624	Queen Nzinga of the Ndongo begins resistance to Portuguese rule
1640s	English transport African slaves to work on sugar plantations in Caribbean colonies
c.1680s	West African kingdoms of Oyo and Dahomey begin to supply about 20,000 slaves a year to European slave traders
1698	Triangular slave trade begins
1713	British gain control of slave trade to Spanish America
1780	Transatlantic slave trade peaks: up to 100,000 Africans exported as slaves annually
1802	Denmark bans Danes from involvement in slave trade
1807	Britain declares slave trade illegal
1808	US bans import of slaves
1812	Slave trade illegal in Mexico, Argentina, Chile, and Venezuela
1815	France abolishes slave trade
1820	Spain abolishes slave trade in colonies but does not enforce
1833	Slave trade banned in British Empire
1846	Slave trade between Portuguese Africa and Brazil at peak
1849	Libreville founded for freed slaves (Gabon)
1865	Thirteenth Amendment: US abolishes slavery
1873	Tippu Tip's central African slave empire flourishes
1880	Slavery ends in Spanish colonies
1882	Portugal bans export of slaves from African colonies; Atlantic slave trade ends

Slavery In Ancient Egypt

This illustration is based on part of a relief from the Saqqara tomb of Haremhab, now in Bologna, Italy, which was discovered in the late 19th century. The relief probably dates from the reign of Tutankhamun, and depicts black slaves under the harsh control of their Egyptian masters.

© DIAGRAM

Trading networks

Into the depths (above)
An African slave takes his first tentative steps in preparation for an arduous voyage across the Atlantic Ocean to serve out his unfortunate destiny in the Americas.

By the 16th century, Europeans had established colonies in the Americas and the Caribbean. Initially, they used Native Americans or European convicts to labor in the mines and on plantations, but many died from disease or cruelty. The Europeans then turned to Africa as a source of slaves, believing that Africans would withstand tropical diseases and harsh conditions.

The Spanish and Portuguese were the first Europeans to engage in the slave trade. They set up trading posts and forts along the coast and began buying slaves from African merchants. The Portuguese traded with the Kongo and Ndongo Kingdoms, sometimes starting wars to produce prisoners of war who could be bought as slaves. By 1502 they were shipping Africans as slaves to Spanish and Portuguese colonies in the Caribbean and Brazil; by the end of the century, an average of 5,000 to 10,000 slaves were leaving Luanda annually for Brazil. The Dutch, French, and British followed, and by the early 18th century, Britain dominated the trade.

A well-established network of trade routes already existed in sub-Saharan Africa. African kingdoms had established long-distance trade in various commodities and the European traders tapped into these routes. Luanda became a Portuguese colony, and slave trading communities developed along Kongo trade routes.

Some slaves originated from relatively short distances from the coast. Trading agents went deep into western Central Africa, however, roaming the interior and buying slaves from local chiefs in exchange for cloth, guns, and other European goods. Many slaves came from inland kingdoms, such as the Luba and Lunda kingdoms.

Various African peoples, such as the Yaka, Imbangala, Teke, and Ovimbundu engaged in the slave trade. The Ovimbundu kingdom, which lay between the coast and the peoples of the interior, was

Reluctant to go! (above)
A slave trader in Zanzibar prepares to buy a mother and child for transportation to potential markets in the Middle or Far East.

particularly well-placed, and the Ovimbundu acted as middlemen in the slave trade, which became a major element of their economy until the early 20th century. The Imbangala people created the kingdom of Kasenje, which in time also became a slave-trading center.

Factors, or traders, who lived in the area, dealt with local African rulers through a network of European and African traders who took a proportion of the goods traded. African merchants brought captured slaves from the interior to the coast in groups of up to 150 Africans, who were chained together and marched on foot to coastal trading posts where they were sold to European traders. Once purchased, the Africans were often branded and imprisoned in the forts while they were waiting to be shipped across the Atlantic.

According to one estimate, between the late 16th century and 1836, some 4 million Africans from Angola alone were captured for the slave trade, only about 2 million of whom survived the march to the coast, the temporary confinement in ports, and the final journey across the Atlantic.

Slave purchasers developed preferences for specific African peoples and ethnic stereotypes developed that would later develop racist stereotypes. For example, traders believed that the Akan peoples of what is now Ghana were rebellious, while Mandingo people from Senegal were considered to be good house servants.

Goods, such as guns, iron bars, cloth, and alcohol were traded for slaves. According to records dated 1756, one African man could be traded for 115 gallons (435 liters) of rum, while a woman was traded for 95 gallons (360 liters). Gold was also used to purchase slaves.

Where the slaves came from

These four maps show the peoples, kingdoms and regions which provided people for the slave trade, or from where they were transported across the Atlantic, during the following periods:
(**1**) Sources 1450–1700;
(**2**) Depots 1450–1700;
(**3**) Sources 1700–1810;
(**4**) Depots 1700–1810.

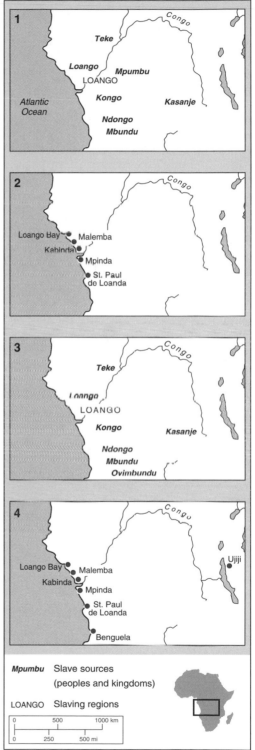

Mpumbu   Slave sources
(peoples and kingdoms)

LOANGO   Slaving regions

0   500   1000 km
0   250   500 mi

© DIAGRAM

Transatlantic trade

Memories of home
On this map of North and South America, and the area of the Caribbean, the tinted areas represent the places to which African slaves were taken. Contemporary diet, religion, music, language, and folk tales all bear witness to a rich African cultural heritage.

Slaves were taken from coastal forts and crammed into ships to be transported across the Atlantic. The Portuguese nicknamed the slave ships *tumbeiros*, meaning coffins.

The journey across the Atlantic took three to six weeks, or even longer, and conditions on board were appalling. Africans were packed into confined quarters, head to toe, often on their sides to save space. There was little ventilation or sanitation and rarely room to stand up. Dysentery and smallpox were commonplace. It was said that people could smell slave ships coming into harbor.

In the early years of the transatlantic trade, between 25–40 percent of the slaves died during the crossing from disease or starvation. Some committed suicide by throwing themselves overboard; some were thrown overboard for acts of resistance. However, the slave trade was highly profitable. The loss of a slave meant loss of profits for the traders, and there were attempts to keep as many alive as possible.

"The triangular trade"

The Atlantic crossing was known as the middle passage in what was effectively a triangular trade. Ships left European ports, such as Bristol or Lisbon, with goods for trade that included guns, iron, cloth, and alcohol.

The ships arrived on the West African coast, where the goods were unloaded and traded for slaves. From Africa, the same ships then set off across the Atlantic laden with slaves for the American and Caribbean colonies.

Slaves were unloaded and sold, and the ships then left the colonies for Europe, with cargoes of gold, tobacco, cotton, molasses, and other goods, which were much in demand in Europe. Having sold on these goods, traders then began the route again.

Not all traders followed this triangular routine. Some crossed directly from the Americas or the Caribbean to the African coast to pick up slaves, then returned directly to the colonies with their human cargo.

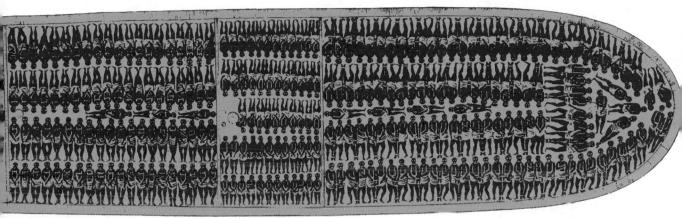

Coffin ships
This illustration graphically portrays the inhumanely cramped
conditions in which African slaves were transported across the
Atlantic Ocean. Not surprisingly, many did not survive the arduous
journey to the European colonies of the so-called "New World."

The "triangular trade" – routes and currents
The thin arrows show the main routes followed by ships involved in
"the triangular trade;" these routes also followed the general
direction of the main currents – the Gulf Stream, and the Canary and
North Equatorial currents.

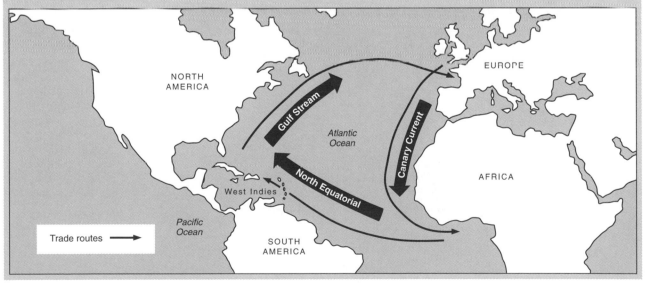

The end of slavery

The slave trade was highly profitable for traders and plantation owners. European ports, such as Bristol, made huge profits from "the triangular trade," and slavery itself became an integral part of the plantation economy in the southern states of North America. As a result, it was many years before the trade ended. Slave traders and plantation owners justified the trade on grounds of race, arguing that Africans were inferior humans, an attitude that created racist prejudice, which exists to the present day.

The move to abolish slavery began as early as 1680 when Quakers in the colony of Pennsylvania condemned slavery on humanitarian grounds. Following American independence from Britain in 1783, slavery became a major issue in the United States and some slaves were freed, particularly in the north. Slaves also resisted their condition and there were slave revolts in the Caribbean, some fueled by the ideas of the French Revolution.

During the 19th century, the abolitionist movement gathered momentum in both Britain and the United States. Former slaves in the Americas joined with whites to fight for the end of slavery. The issue of slavery led to a civil war in the United States, which ended in 1865 with the abolition of slavery.

In the 19th century, first Denmark, then Britain, France, and Spain finally banned the slave trade. In what is now Gabon, French colonists established a settlement known

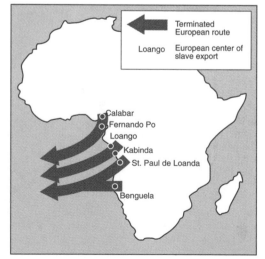

Ending the trade
This map shows the extent to which the inhuman slave trade was suppressed, in the period before 1870, from the ports of Benguela, St. Paul de Loanda, Kabinda, Loango, Fernando Po, and Calabar on the western coast of Central Africa.

as Libreville for freed slaves. However, some traders, such as Zanzibar merchant Tippu Tip, who had a private slaving empire in Central Africa, continued to supply slaves, and the Atlantic trade did not finally come to an end until the 1880s.

Effects of the trade

The slave trade made some local African chiefs enormously wealthy but, ultimately, the trade undermined local economies and political stability, and many African villages lost their labor force, which was shipped overseas. The population of what is now the Central African Republic, for instance, was greatly reduced. According to some calculations, if the slave trade had not occurred, Africa's population in the 19th century would have been double what it was. Slave raids and civil wars between different African groups were also commonplace. The Kongo and Ndongo kingdoms, for example, experienced complete cultural disintegration and political collapse.

Incursions by slave traders opened a foothold for European colonists who arrived on the African continent during the late 19th century. In some cases, such as the Belgian Congo, brutal treatment of Africans under the slave trade opened the way to later atrocities.

Enlightenment
This emblem is a late 18th-century expression of public opinion, effectively mobilized by abolitionists, in opposition to the slave trade.

The slave trade and the abolition of slavery: 1815–1873

1815 **France:** Slave trade in its colonies banned during Napoleon's Hundred Days' administration. **Portugal:** Slave trade in its colonies in northern hemisphere banned, with the ban extended to all colonies in 1830.

1820 **Spain:** Slave trade in all its colonies banned.

1822 **Britain:** Agreement concluded with sultan of Zanzibar (center of Arab trade in slaves), restricting East African slave trade. Second agreement (1846) further restricts the trade.

1823 **Britain:** Anti-Slavery Society established; it is dedicated to a worldwide ban on slavery

1830 **South America:** Most states achieve independence from Spanish rule and abolish slavery, or adopt programs of gradual emancipation.

1833 **Britain:** Slavery banned in all its colonies.

1848 **France:** Slavery banned in all its colonies by French provisional government following the establishment of the 2nd Republic.

1863 **US:** President Lincoln issues Emancipation Proclamation freeing all slaves in US (in practice, it was effective only in areas controlled by Union army).

1865 **US:** End of American Civil War. 13th Amendment to US constitution abolishes slavery.

1870 **Spain:** Policy of gradual slave emancipation adopted on Caribbean island of Cuba (the largest remaining center of slave use in Spanish colonial possessions).

1873 **Britain:** Now a dominant power in East Africa, Britain forces Sultan of Zanzibar to ban slave trade in his dominions, effectively ending East African slave trade from Zanzibar.

© DIAGRAM

LUBA-LUNDA STATES

While the Kongo and Ndongo kingdoms flourished on the western coastal area of Central Africa, a number of important kingdoms were developing farther inland. One was the Luba kingdom, which was founded in the 16th century. From this emerged a complex of other states and kingdoms, sometimes known as the Luba-Lunda states, as they shared similar political structures.

The major offshoot of the Luba kingdom was the Lunda Empire, which began in the 1600s. The Lunda adopted and developed the Luba system of government, expanded their territory, and gave rise to a number of other kingdoms or states, which spread into the south Congo Basin, and what are now western Angola, and Zambia.

Both the Luba kingdom and the Lunda Empire had strong, centralized government headed by powerful kings, and they dominated the central grasslands of the Congo region and Zambia.

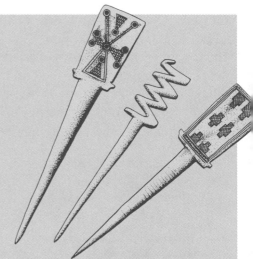

Ivory pendant (left)
This piece of jewelry is a type of *mikisi mihasi*, a sculpture named for revered ancestors.

Hairpins (above)
Made from ivory, these antique hairpins are usually embellished with designs which are painted in natural pigments. They date from the late 19th century.

42

State development reached a peak in the 18th and 19th century. Offshoots of the Lunda Empire included the Kazembe kingdom and the Lozi of western Zambia, who created a unified kingdom from a number of smaller chiefdoms. The Bemba, descendants of the Luba, also founded a small kingdom in what is now Zambia that expanded greatly during the 18th and 19th centuries. Other important states were those of the Ovimbundu in what is now Angola, and the Kuba kingdom.

During the 19th century states fluctuated in size, with some declining while others, such as the Ovimbundu, expanded. Most were merchant states who supplied European and Muslim traders with slaves and ivory.

An undignified end
In 1895 the Chokwe invaded the Lunda territories from Angola in the north. Defeated Chokwe soldiers were first decapitated, and then their skulls were impaled on poles as a warning to any other potential invaders in the future.

Central African kingdoms (below)
This map shows the principal empires, kingdoms or states in Central Africa in 1880.

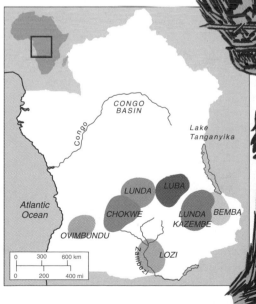

© DIAGRAM

Luba kingdom

One of the most powerful states in Central Africa, the Luba kingdom had its origins in a number of chieftainships that existed in the Katanga region of southeastern Congo in the 14th century. People had probably been living in the region for many centuries, and historians believe that the idea of rule by chiefs began there as early as the eighth century.

Population pressure and shortage of land led to conflict between the various chieftainships, and larger military groupings emerged. The most powerful was the Luba group from around the Lake Kisale area.

According to oral tradition the Songye, who had come from the north, were the first to rule the Luba, or Kalundwe as they were then called. The Songye ruler, or *kongolo*, married the Kalundwe queen and set up a new state, which became the Luba kingdom. Its territory stretched between the Lualaba and Lubilash rivers.

In the 15th century the Kunda, who came from the north and were led by Mbili Kiluhe, displaced the Songye rulers. Mbili Kiluhe married two of the reigning *kongolo's* sisters. His son, Kalo Ilungu, became a great warrior and, claiming matrilineal descent, challenged and defeated the reigning *kongolo*. He was the founder of the Kunda dynasty, which ruled the Luba kingdom until the late 19th century.

Bowstand
This is an example of the bowstands retained by Luba rulers both as a symbol of their authority, and to commemorate the founder of their dynasty, Mbili Kiluhe, who was a famous hunter.

Luba chief (right)
The Luba kingdom consisted of provinces, which in turn comprised groups of chiefdoms. Each province had its own chief, who was appointed by the king, or by or one of his subordinates.

Strong government

By the mid-16th century, the Luba kingdom was a powerful state with a strong, centralized government, under a king known as the *mulopwe*, who had more power than any chiefs before him in that region. The king was head of state and spiritual leader and ruled with a group of ministers, or *balopwe*. Each minister had specific duties and was descended from Kala Ilunga, so creating a small ruling aristocracy, or elite. Ministers included the *sungu*, who was effectively a prime minister and passed on messages between the king and chiefs, the *nsikala*, who acted as temporary ruler when the king was absent, and the *inabanza* who looked after ritual matters. The *twite* commanded the army and a special police-like force. A pyramid of power therefore existed, with the king in position at its summit. He ruled from the capital of the kingdom, and received tribute from conquered chiefs.

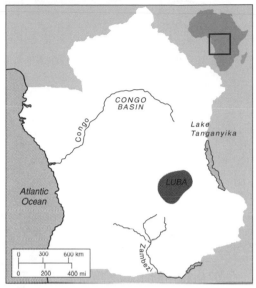

Where it was (above)
This map shows the geographical location of the Luba kingdom within the region of Central Africa in 1880.

Settlement (below)
This illustration represents a military settlement in Manyema, a northeastern province of the Luba kingdom, in the 1870s.

© DIAGRAM

45

Lunda empire

An Ovimbundu staff (above)
A status symbol plus walking aid, the craftsmanship of this staff attests to the rise of powerful Angolan chiefdoms in the 16th–17th centuries.

Chiefs and others who failed to gain power in the Luba kingdom often left to form new kingdoms. Around 1600 a Luba chief, called Kibinda Ilunga, the brother of the ruling king, left the Luba kingdom and moved westward, where he founded what was to become the Lunda Empire.

The Lunda people occupied small territories in what is now the southern region of the Democratic Republic of Congo. Kibinda Ilunga married the Lunda's senior chief, a woman called Lueji, and became paramount chief. His son, Lusengi, introduced the Luba methods of government, and his grandson, Naweji, began conquering new lands. By 1700 the Lunda Empire had a capital, Mussumba, a tax-gathering system run by provincial administrators, and a king bearing the title Mwata Yamvo, or emperor of the Lunda.

The hierarchy of government, from emperor down through various levels of chiefs, was modeled on the Luba system. Subject peoples paid tributes to the emperor, who in return provided military protection; their territories were incorporated into the empire and conquered chiefs were made Lunda chiefs, although they kept some of their power, making the Lunda system more stable than the Luba system.

The Lunda became the largest and most successful of the merchant empires. They were well-placed on existing east-west trading routes and, as the empire expanded, their commercial networks spread east and west as far as the lower Zambezi and the Indian Ocean. Their wealth came from ivory, copper, and slaves, which they traded with Arabs in the east and Portuguese in the west.

Kazembe kingdom

During the 17th century, the Luba-Lunda political system spread outward to west and east, as chiefs migrated from the original territories and formed new kingdoms. One leader, Kinguri, led his people into what is now Angola, where they took the name *Imbangala*, formed an alliance with traders, and set up a trading kingdom on the Kasenje plain.

The largest and most successful Luba-Lunda offshoot was the Kazembe kingdom, in what is now Zambia. It began in the late 17th century when the Lunda emperor rewarded one of his chiefs by giving the man's son (Ngonda Bilonda) the title Mwata Kazembe, and sending him to lead an expansion eastward. Bilonda's son became ruler of lands east of the Lualaba River and his successors expanded the kingdom, acquiring wealth through trade and tribute. By 1800 the Kazembe's capital was at the heart of trade routes across the continent.

Kazembe IV
This is a portrait of Kibangu Keleka, who ruled the Lunda empire during the period 1805–1850.

Ndumba Tembo
He was the chief of the Chokwe who, in 1895, invaded Lunda territory and assumed control of the capital.

Political collapse

During the 19th century, the Lunda empire was weakened by wars and invasions. In 1895 the Chokwe, governed by the Lunda kings, invaded Lunda territory and took over the capital. By the late 19th century, Europeans had colonized all the Lunda territory and, by 1900, the independent kingdom of Kazembe had ceased to exist.

© DIAGRAM

Bemba and Lozi kingdoms

Where it was (below)
This map shows the geographical location of the Bemba kingdom within Central Africa in 1880.

"Crocodile Clan" (right)
This was the name given to the Bena Yanda, one of the Bemba groups who migrated from the Congo into Zambia.

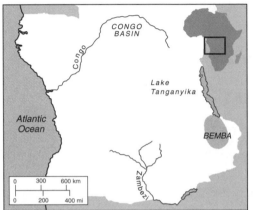

An audience with the king (below)
This meeting between the British explorer and missionary, David Livingstone, and the Bemba king, *Chitimukulu* Chitapankwa, took place in January 1867.

From the 17th century the Luba-Lunda system of government spread into what is now Zambia where, as well as the Kazembe kingdom, two powerful kingdoms developed – the Bemba and the Lozi kingdoms

Bemba kingdom

The Bemba migrated from the Katanga region of the Congo into northern Zambia where they conquered, or absorbed, the original inhabitants. Led by a chief called Chiti, one of the migrant groups, the *Bena Yanda*, who were probably descended from Lunda chiefs, settled on the banks of the Chambeshi river in about 1650.

Like other Lunda states, the Bemba were ruled by a king. His title was *Chitimukulu*, meaning Chiti the Great. The kingdom, which started small, expanded steadily during the 18th and 19th centuries. The Bemba territory was rich in minerals and, in the late 19th century, it was taken over by the British South Africa Company (BSAC).

An historic celebration
The movement of the Lozi king between capitals, at the annual flooding of the Zambezi river, is celebrated during the Kuomboka Festival. The event dates back to the founding of the kingdom in the 18th century.

Lozi kingdom

The Lozi kingdom developed in western Zambia. Led by a woman, Mwambwe, the Lozi, or Luyi, migrated from the north in about the 17th century. Mwambe was succeeded by her daughter, and then her grandson, Mboo, who became the first Lozi king, or *litunga*. Under Mboo's rule, the Lozi kingdom, which at that stage consisted of semi-independent chiefdoms, expanded its territory, conquering and absorbing neighboring peoples.

During the early 18th century, the reigning *litunga*, Ngalama, began to unify the chiefdoms on Luba-Lunda lines, establishing a hierarchy of power from king through layers of chiefs. The Bemba ruler Mulambwa (who reigned during the period c. 1780–1830) completed the process of unification, and also set up direct rule over conquered groups and new migrants.

The kingdom prospered under Mulambwa's rule. Migrant groups arrived, including the Mbunda from Angola, who settled on the borders and helped to defend the kingdom. The Mbunda introduced bows and arrows and a new type of battleax, and new crops to the region, such as cassava, millet, and yams.

After Mulambwe's death, there were arguments over who should succeed him. Civil war broke out, which weakened the kingdom. The Kololo, from southern Africa, attacked and conquered the kingdom, ruling it until the Lozi, under Sipopa, regained power. The kingdom flourished for some years but, by 1900, British imperialists had taken control.

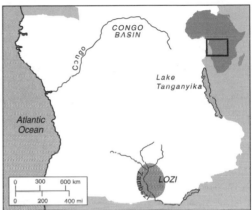

Where it was (above)
This map shows the location of the Lozi kingdom in Central Africa in 1880.

A question of balance
King Lewanika of the Lozi meets with the British South Africa Company in Lealui, the capital city, to discuss trading concessions.

© DIAGRAM

49

"People of the Throwing Knife"

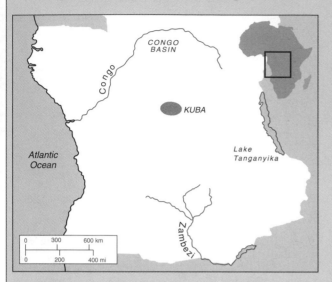

Where it was (above)
This map shows the geographical location of the Kuba kingdom within the region of Central Africa in 1880.

During the 16th century, the Kuba people, Bantu-speakers who had lived in the Congo Basin since about the third century, moved from the lower Basin to the Kasai region. They migrated partly to escape Jaga invasions, and partly to move away from Portuguese influence.

Gradually, a powerful Kuba state developed, led by the Bushongo, a name meaning "People of the Throwing Knife." Originally fishing people, they grew wealthy from growing corn and tobacco. By the early 18th century, they had established a flourishing economy and a stable government, with a ruling aristocratic class headed by a king.

The wealthy Kuba kingdom contained skilled artisans. Trade developed and the Kuba exported luxury cloth and ivory, and imported beads, copper, salt, and slaves. Ultimately, the Kuba controlled many of the trade routes in Central Africa.

The kingdom flourished throughout the 18th century and well into the 19th. It was politically and economically stable and not as affected by the slave trade as many other kingdoms. In the late 19th century, however, the kingdom suffered wars and was invaded by the Nsapo people. As a result, the kingdom was broken up to a large extent. Europeans arrived in the area in 1884 and, a year later, the Kuba were incorporated into the private colony of Léopold II, king of Belgium.

Throwing knife (above left)
Typical of the Bwaka people of Central Africa, this steel knife is engraved on the blades, and bound at the grip on the handle. Such knives turn around the center of gravity in-flight, and can cut or pierce the intended victim at almost any angle of impact.

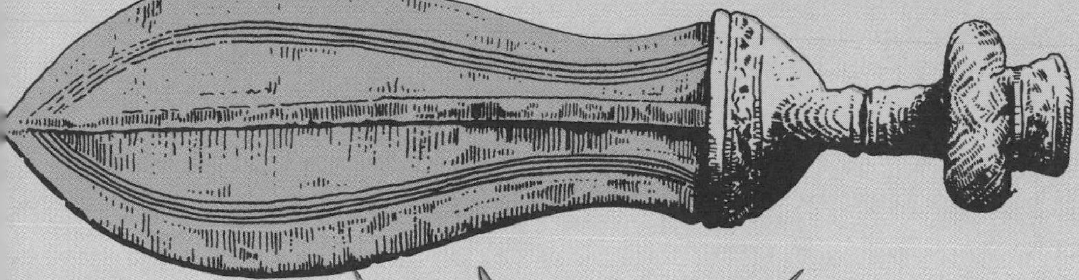

Ikula knife
In stark contrast to the deadly throwing knife (see below left), this wooden peace knife was introduced in the early 17th century.

Bope Mabinshe
A modern Kuba monarch, he is shown here at his coronation in 1947. Ruling his kingdom by the doctrine of divine right, he was typical of the Kuba kings who preceded him in his attitude toward his subjects. He died in 1969.

Kot aPe
He was the ruler of the Kuba kingdom at the beginning of the 20th century.

© DIAGRAM

51

"SCRAMBLE" FOR CENTRAL AFRICA

Colonial involvement: 1472–1908

1472	Portugal claims island of Bioko
1485	Portuguese begin colonizing São Tomé and Príncipe
1576	Portuguese build fort at Luanda, and begin colonizing Angola
1807	Britain outlaws Atlantic slave trade
1839	France sets up trading post, later Libreville (Gabon)
1845–1858	Spain creates colony of Spanish Guinea (Equatorial Guinea)
1849	Freed slaves are settled in Libreville, Gabon
1852–1873	David Livingstone explores Central and East Africa
1855	Livingstone reaches Victoria Falls, Zambia
1874–1877	Henry Morton Stanley explores Congo River
1875	Pierre Savorgnan de Brazza explores Congo region
1880s	Lunda Empire breaks up
1880	France colonizes region north of Congo River
1884–1885	Berlin Conference recognizes King Leopold's claim to Congo, French claim to Gabon, and Portuguese control of Angola
1889	Gabon becomes part of French colony of Middle Congo
1890	British South Africa Company (BSAC) make Lozi kingdom (Zambia) part of their Rhodesian colony
1891	Colony of French Congo set up
1894	French create colony of Oubangoui–Shari
1897–1900	BSAC conquer Bemba kingdom, which becomes part of Northern Rhodesia
1899	British conquer Kazembe kingdom
1902–1903	Ballundo War: Africans resist Portuguese colonization of Angola
1908	Belgian government takes over Congo Free State, which is renamed Belgian Congo

Berlin Conference 1884–1885
European heads of state attended a conference in Berlin, Germany, to sort out their claims to territory in Africa. Decisions were made without the consent of the Africans.

From the mid-19th century, huge changes took place in Central Africa. Explorers such as David Livingstone and Henry Morton Stanley opened up the region. They were closely followed by, or worked with, colonizers – British, French, and Belgians – who, from the 1880s, divided up and colonized Central Africa as part of what was known as the "scramble" for Africa.

Berlin Conference
Before 1880 European colonial rule in Central Africa was limited to the Portuguese dependency of Angola, São Tomé and Príncipe, and the French coastal colony of Gabon (founded 1845). Initially European involvement was motivated largely by the slave trade. Once this ended, there were other motives. These included a rising demand for new products, such as rubber, and imperialism, the wish to create foreign empires, or obtain foreign possessions. Belgium was one of the first colonizers in the region beginning in 1876, and France and Britain were not far behind. The European desire for African colonies caused conflict within Africa, and rivalry between the European powers, each of whom sought a stake in the continent.

Division of a continent
By 1913 not only Central Africa but the entire continent had come under European control. These maps show the extent of expansion by the five major colonial powers at four critical dates: 1884, 1891, 1895, and 1912.

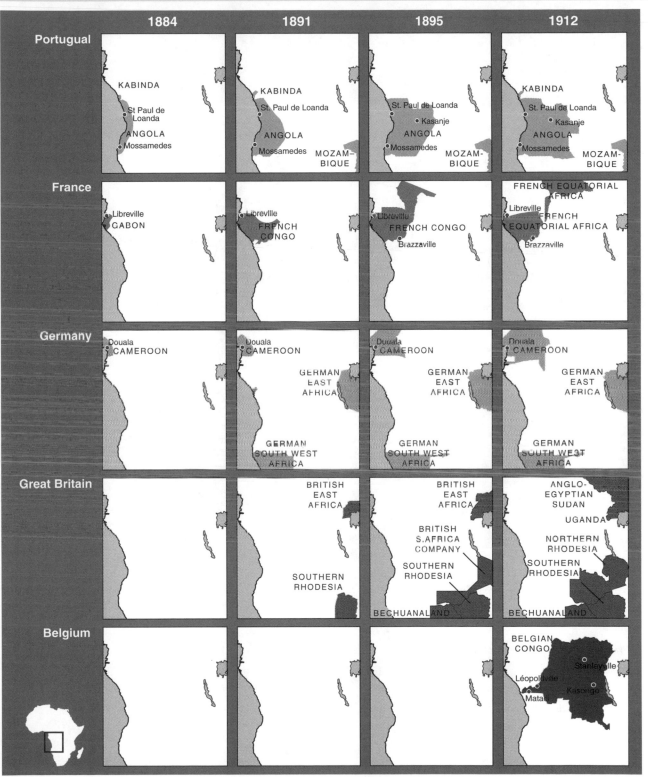

© DIAGRAM

Explorers and missionaries 1

Exploring the interior of Central Africa

1850s	Paul B. Du Chaillu explores lower Ogooué River (Gabon)
1851	Livingstone reaches what is now Zambia
1852–1873	David Livingstone explores Central and East Africa
1855	Livingstone visits Victoria Falls, Zambia
1860s	A.M.A. Aymes explores lower Ogooué River (Gabon)
1870	Georg August Schweinfurth reaches Azande territory (Central African Republic)
1874–1877	Henry Morton Stanley explores Congo River
1875	Pierre Savorgnan de Brazza explores Congo region
1877	Stanley reaches mouth of the Oubangui River (Central African Republic)
1880	de Brazza founds Franceville, later Brazzaville (Gabon)
1913	Albert Schweitzer establishes hospital at Lambaréné on Ogooué River (Gabon)

End of an era
G. Schweinfurth reached the Mangbetu kingdom in 1870. This illustration, based on his sketch, shows King Munza's reception hall. The African greatness he witnessed was soon to be overshadowed by the encroaching colonial powers.

Until the 19th century Europeans knew very little about the interior of Central Africa. However, from the 1850s missionaries and explorers began to penetrate the interior. Their reasons varied from the wish to convert Africans to Christianity, to the ambition for scientific discovery. Some, such as Livingstone, also worked to end the slave trade.

The knowledge that explorers brought back was of great interest to European powers keen to tap into Africa's huge resources and acquire new territory. From the mid-19th century, several European powers sent expeditions into Central Africa to claim exclusive rights over territory.

Exploring the Congo Basin

The Portuguese reached the mouth of the Congo River in the 15th century, but the great age of African exploration did not take place until the 19th century. Between 1800 and 1880, various explorers traced the course of Central African rivers, reaching and opening up areas that Europeans had never seen before.

David Livingstone

Probably the greatest explorer of the period was David Livingstone. A medical student, he was also a missionary with a burning ambition to convert Africans to Christianity.

He arrived in Africa in 1841 and, from 1849, combined his evangelical aims with exploration. In 1851 he located the course of the upper Zambezi River, then headed west and reached Luanda. He set off again to follow the Zambezi River downstream, reaching the Victoria Falls in 1855, and journeying as far as the Indian Ocean. He was the first European to cross southern Africa from west to east

From 1866 he made further journeys in an attempt to find the source of the Nile, reaching Ujiji near Lake Tanganyika in 1871. Livingstone died two years later, having not only mapped the courses of the Zambezi and Lualaba rivers but also having helped to end the Arab slave trade.

Explorers and missionaries 2

Ingenuity
An American journalist and explorer, Henry Morton Stanley (left) traveled sometimes aboard a five-sectioned portable boat called *Lady Alice* (right). It was carried 2,000 miles overland, and sailed 4,000 miles on his descent of the Congo in 1877.

Creating the French Congo (below)
Pierre Savorgnan de Brazza, the explorer, is entertained at the court of the Teke king prior to signing the treaty in 1882 which made the territory north of the Congo River a French protectorate.

During the 1870s and 1880s European powers sent expeditions into Central Africa specifically to acquire territory. Some were backed up with military force.

One of the most ambitious explorers was the American, Henry Morton Stanley. He was first sent to Africa as a reporter for the *New York Herald*, with the task of searching for David Livingstone, who had disappeared. The two men met in 1871. Subsequently Stanley undertook a major expedition, tracing the course of the Congo River to the sea, and reaching the Oubangui River in 1877. In 1879–1884 the Belgian king, Léopold II, hired him and sent him back to the Congo to carve out a colony. Stanley founded a number of stations along the middle Congo River and signed treaties with African kings, setting up the Congo Free State for Léopold.

French Equatorial Africa
Meanwhile Pierre Savorgnan de Brazza was also investigating the Congo region, around the Ogooué River in what is now Gabon. Employed by the French government, de Brazza navigated the river upstream, stopping just short of the River Congo. In 1879 he

A man with a mission (below)
Born in Germany in 1875, Albert Schweitzer made the decision in 1896 that he would live for science and art until he reached the age of 30, after which time he would devote his life to the service of humanity.

Fully qualified as a missionary doctor, he and and his wife, a trained nurse, set up a hospital to combat leprosy at Lambaréné, in the heart of French Equatorial Africa, in 1913.

Despite setbacks, not least of which were the disruption caused by two World Wars, and also strong opposition from missionary societies that disagreed with his theological views, he continued his work until his death, at the age of 90, in 1965.

returned to the region. In 1880 be founded Franceville (later Brazzaville) and negotiated a treaty with the African king, Makoko, giving sovereignty of the region on the north bank of the Congo River to France, so helping to create what became French Equatorial Africa.

Missionary activity

During the 19th century, missionaries were active throughout Central Africa and, in the early 19th century, many also worked against slavery. Missions were set up in what are now Gabon and the Congo republics and, by 1914, Christian missions had been founded throughout Africa. The church continued to play an important role throughout the colonial era, and was active in providing basic schooling and hospitals. The Roman Catholic church was particularly active in the Belgian colony and eventually founded a university, which provided training for white colonists and a small elite of black Africans. The most famous missionary of all was Albert Schweitzer who, with his wife, moved to Lambaréné on the banks of the Ogooué River in French Equatorial Africa. They founded a self-financed hospital.

A private Belgian colony

No escape!
A contemporary, satirical cartoon portrays the dilemma of an African worker in the Congo Free State who is forced to increase the output of rubber for his colonial master, King Léopold II of Belgium.

The Belgian king, Léopold II, led European colonization of Central Africa. He created his own personal colony in what is now the Democratic Republic of the Congo. Under his rule, it was known as the Congo Free State.

Léopold II believed the Congo had great economic potential and began colonizing the region in the late 1870s. He sent Henry Morton Stanley to the Congo Basin to establish his authority and to set up the colony, which he did between 1879 and 1884. At that time the Congo had no overall political unity. Instead, there were a number of powerful Arab, Swahili, and Nyamwezi rulers engaged in trade. They included Muhammad bin Hamad, known as Tippu Tip, a Swahili Arab trader who ruled a large part of the eastern Congo and Msiri, a Nyamwezi ruler, who was also a major force in the region.

At the Conference of Berlin, European powers recognized Léopold's claim to the Congo Basin and, in 1885, he announced the establishment of the Congo Free State with himself as King Sovereign of the colony. Katanga, the mineral-rich heartland of the Luba kingdom, was incorporated into the colony. During the early 1890s, local rulers such as Msiri were either killed or, in the case of Tippu Tip, made administrators of the colony.

Atrocities

Effectively a dictator, Léopold made a fortune from exploiting Congolese rubber. To finance his colonial venture, he rented out areas of land to commercial companies, such as the Antwerp Company, the Anglo-Belgian India Rubber Company, and the *Compagnie du Katange*, who were licenced to make profits and pay tributes and tax to him.

The Congolese people suffered dreadfully and atrocities were committed as locals were forced to give up farming to collect the sap needed to produce rubber. Workers who failed to produce enough were beaten with a *chicotte*, a whip made from sun-dried hippo hide, and mutilation of arms, hands, or feet was a common punishment for workers accused of theft or other offences. It has been estimated that between 1880 and 1920 the population of the colony halved. One estimate suggests that 10 million Congolese died from murder, starvation, and disease.

Conditions in the Congo caused outrage in Belgium and an international outcry. The Irish diplomat and nationalist Roger Casement did much to expose the atrocities and, in 1908, the Belgian government annexed the colony and renamed it the Belgian Congo.

Massacre (above)
Under Léopold II's rule, the Congolese people suffered many atrocities, one of which was the massacre of the Manyema women at Nyangwe on July 15, 1871.

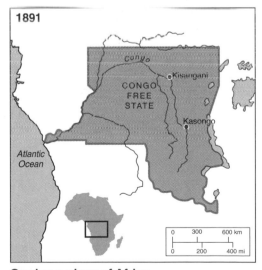

Owning a piece of Africa
This map shows the area occupied by the Congo Free State in 1891. It was claimed as the personal possession of King Léopold II of Belgium, and administered in a ruthless manner by his unscrupulous agents.

© DIAGRAM

The French Congo

During the nineteenth century, the French established a number of colonies in Central Africa, which stretched from what is now Gabon, through the Republic of the Congo, and northeast to the Central African Republic, which was then called Ubangi-Shari. Between 1897–1910, all the French colonies in Central Africa were known collectively under the name of The French Congo.

By the late 18th century the French became involved in the slave trade. In 1815 the Congress of Vienna abolished the trade, but slaves continued to be exported from the Gabon coast. French naval patrols worked successfully to reduce the numbers. In 1839 the French founded a settlement for freed slaves on the Gabon coast which, in 1849, was named Libreville, meaning Free Town in English.

Between 1843–1886 French naval officers administered the area. Towards the end of the period, the French began to explore the interior. As with Belgium, exploration was linked to colonization. During the 1870s the explorers Georg August Schweinfurth and Henry Morton Stanley began to open up what is now the Central African Republic, and in the 1880s Pierre Savorgnan de Brazza paved the way for French colonization.

In 1880 de Brazza founded a trading post at Franceville, which later became known as Brazzaville, in what is now southeastern Gabon. In 1882 he negotiated a treaty with the Teke king, Ilo Makoko, to establish a French colony on the north bank of the Congo River. It became known as French Congo. In 1903 the territory was renamed Middle Congo, by which time it also included Gabon.

Moving farther north, in 1889, the French authorities established an outpost at Bangui and, in 1894, they created a territory called Ubangi-(Oubangi)-Shari, which is now known as the Central African Republic.

King Makoko
He was the Teke king who, in 1882, negotiated a treaty with the French explorer, Pierre Savorgnan de Brazza, to establish a French colony on the north bank of the Congo River in what is now known as Gabon.

A noble cause
This stamp, issued in 1931, reinforced the view that France was a civilizing influence on African nations.

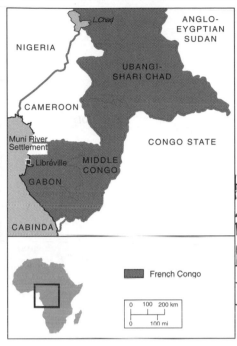

Colonies in Africa (above left)
During the period 1897–1910 the area known as the French Congo comprised Gabon, Middle Congo, Ubangi-Shari, and Chad.

Raising the flag (above right)
Makoko, a local ruler, granted the French colonial authorities rights over an area north of the Congo, and unreservedly continued to support their interests.

Pierre Savorgnan de Brazza
A French explorer, he founded a trading post (in 1880) on the site of what was to become Brazzaville, the capital of French Equatorial Africa, in 1910.

Concessionary companies

France, like Léopold II, used commercial companies to administer its colonial possessions and exploit rubber, ivory, and timber resources. The companies used harsh measures against African workers. In 1905 and 1906, the use of forced labor, and its damaging effect on the population, led to public scandal. Africans put up unsuccessful resistance against ill treatment. In 1907 the French government limited the role of concessionary companies and, in 1910, Ubangi-Shari, the Congo, Gabon and Chad were incorporated into a huge federal region called French Equatorial Africa.

© DIAGRAM

61

The British in Central Africa

Former colony
A stamp issued in 1897 when Nyasaland was still a part of British Central Africa.

Overseas visit
A stamp issued to mark the visit of the British Association, and the opening of the bridge at Victoria Falls.

New status
A stamp issued to mark the change in name to Nyasaland Protectorate.

'The Rhodes Colossus'
This illustration, which was based upon a cartoon in *Punch* magazine, wickedly satirizes the attempts by Cecil Rhodes, founder of the British South Africa Company (BSAC) to expand British dominance throughout the entire continent of Africa.

Britain's main colonial influence on the continent was in Southern Africa but, during the 19th century, it also established colonies in Central Africa, namely Northern Rhodesia (now Zambia) and Nyasaland (now Malawi).

In 1851 the Scottish explorer David Livingstone arrived in what is now Zambia. He was the first European to reach the Victoria Falls in 1855. During the 1880s, agents of Cecil Rhodes' British South Africa Company (BSAC) arrived in the region, which then contained the Lozi and Kazembe kingdoms, as well as Ngoni chieftainships. The BSAC took over administration of the region, either signing treaties with African leaders, including Lewinaka, king of the Lozi, or conquering rulers by force. Subsequently the territory was divided into Northwestern and Northeastern Rhodesia until 1911, when the two were joined into one area called Northern Rhodesia.

The BSAC meanwhile had been granted a charter to colonize much of central southern Africa, including not only Northern Rhodesia but also the areas which are now known as Zimbabwe and Malawi.

Livingstone arrived in what is now Malawi in 1859, where he witnessed wars and suffering that had been caused by the slave trade. He introduced Christianity to the region and, in 1875, the Free Church of Scotland set up a mission. In 1891 Britain made the region a colony, which they called Nyasaland. It was later renamed the Central Africa Protectorate until 1907 when its name once again became Nyasaland.

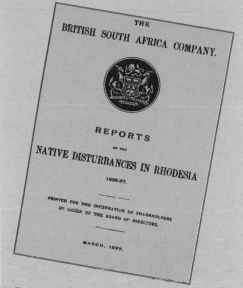

Overseas intelligence
Company reports, such as this one on the sensitive subject of *Native Disturbances in Rhodesia* (March, 1898), were issued for the benefit of shareholders in the British South Africa Company (BSAC).

Receiving a European
Contacts such as this between Europeans and the Bemba led to the Bemba kingdom being incorporated into Northern Rhodesia.

© DIAGRAM

FROM COLONIALISM TO INDEPENDENCE

Forced to fight
Africans were often enlisted to fight in the armies of the European colonial powers during World War I.

Sergeant, Rhodesia Regiment
Citizens in the large towns, together with members of the Southern Rhodesia Volunteers, joined together to form this regiment.

Between 1910 and 1960 the whole of Central Africa was under colonial rule. Colonialism provided schools, hospitals, and transport systems, such as roads and railways, but European rule was often harsh and brutal. African-led trade and trading networks were brought to an end, and colonizers introduced new economic systems to benefit themselves.

In the first phase of colonization, European colonizers had concentrated on forcibly extracting rubber, ivory, and timber, and their efforts were accompanied by considerable violence. In the 20th century, colonizers adopted a more systematic approach to economic re-organization, developing plantation economies, single cash crops, and a lucrative mining industry. The effects on local populations were hard and sometimes brutal: farmers were forced to abandon subsistence ways of living; workers were exploited; families were separated; and famine was common. The emphasis on exploiting raw materials also meant that even today many Central African nations are still dependent on exporting raw materials rather than manufactured goods.

Africans put up continuous resistance to colonization, but it was not until the 1950s that organized nationalist and liberation movements emerged. In 1960 the first Central African nations achieved independence from colonial rule and, by 1975, the whole of the region had regained independence as separate nations.

Independent states
These three maps show the dates on which the nation states in Central Africa became independent from their colonial rulers. The map (left) focuses on 1960; the map (center) covers the period 1961–1969; and the map (right) records the situation between 1970–1975.

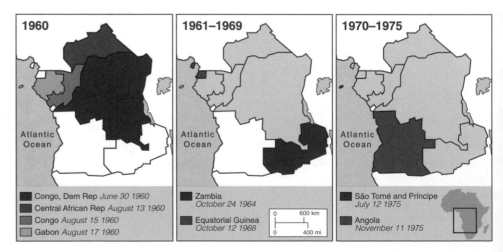

1960

Atlantic Ocean

- Congo, Dem Rep *June 30 1960*
- Central African Rep *August 13 1960*
- Congo *August 15 1960*
- Gabon *August 17 1960*

1961–1969

Atlantic Ocean

- Zambia *October 24 1964*
- Equatorial Guinea *October 12 1968*

0   600 km
0   400 mi

1970–1975

Atlantic Ocean

- São Tomé and Príncipe *July 12 1975*
- Angola *November 11 1975*

Colonial power in Central Africa

1800–1900 BSAC conquer Bemba kingdom, which becomes part of Northern Rhodesia

1884–1885 Berlin Conference

1885 Léopold II, king of Belgium, establishes his own personal colony, which becomes known as the Congo Free State

1890 Barotseland Treaty: British South Africa Company (BSAC) takes over Lozi kingdom as Barotseland, part of Northern Rhodesia

1899 British conquer Kazembe kingdom

1902–1903 Bailundo War: resistance to Portuguese colonization of Angola

1908 Belgian government takes over Congo Free State and renames it the Belgian Congo

1914–1918 World War I

1920s–1930s Copper mining develops in Zambian copperbelt

1923–1924 British government takes control of Southern and Northern Rhodesia

1939–1940 African mineworkers strike for better pay, Northern Rhodesia

1939–1945 World War II

1946 Oubangui–Shari (Central African Republic) and Middle Congo (Republic of Congo and Gabon) become French overseas territories; nationalist movement forms in Northern Rhodesia

1950s Kariba Dam built on Zambezi River

1951 Angola becomes overseas province of Portugal

1953 Northern Rhodesia (Zambia), Southern Rhodesia (Zimbabwe) and Nyasaland (Malawi) merged to form Central African Federation (CAF)

1956 Oubangui–Shari and Middle Congo given internal self–government

1957 Oil discovered in Congo region

1958 Zambia Africa National Congress (ZANC) founded under leadership of Kenneth Kaunda

1960 Belgian Congo achieves independence as Congo; Central African Republic achieves independence; French Congo achieves independence as Congo Republic

1960 South Kasai and Katanga provinces announce secession from Congo; civil war breaks out

1960 Liberation movement begins, São Tomé and Príncipe

1961 Angolan War of Independence begins

1963 Equatorial Guinea gains some self–government; Central African Federation ends

Dauti Yamba (above)
He was the founder of the Zambian Federation of Welfare Societies in Northern Rhodesia (now Zambia) in 1946. These achieved local improvements, such as the construction of new roads and bridges.

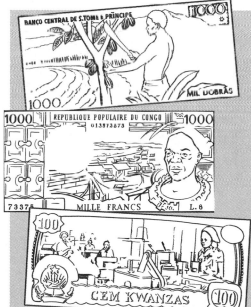

National pride
Banknotes issued by former European colonies which had recently achieved independence reflect a confidence and optimism in their ability to run their own economic affairs with success in the future.

© DIAGRAM

Developing the land

Life for Africans under colonial rule varied but, by and large, they were treated as inferior. European rulers introduced economic changes but they were designed to benefit Europeans, not Africans. Many of the changes caused considerable suffering to the local populations.

Plantation economies

In 1885 the Conference of Berlin awarded the island of Bioko to Spain; in 1900 Spain also gained the area of Rio Muni. Grouped together they made up the colony of Spanish Guinea (now Equatorial Guinea). Economic development was largely confined to Bioko, where cash crops, such as cocoa, timber, and palm oil, were produced. Africans, particularly the Fang, were heavily taxed or forcibly conscripted to labor on plantations. In the 1940s the Spanish developed the economy of Rio Muni. By 1960 about 6,000 Europeans, mainly Spanish, lived in the colony, and controlled cocoa and timber production.

Europeans also developed cocoa plantations on the islands of São Tomé and Príncipe. In 1875 the Portuguese had banned slavery, but plantation owners brought in Africans as contracted laborers from other Portuguese colonies, including Angola. They were regarded in much the same way as slaves and received harsh treatment, leading to periodic revolts. Following one revolt in 1953, the Portuguese killed hundreds of workers in what became known as the Batopa Massacre.

Traveling in style
This illustration is based on a rail from a chieftain's chair, and shows a white colonial officer being carried by his Congolese soldiers. The poles used to carry him are made up from the soldiers' rifles.

Forced labor (right)
Local workers were often forcibly conscripted to work on plantations owned by European colonists. Treated extremely harshly, they had no more rights than slaves, and any opposition to their rulers was swiftly and brutally suppressed.

Angola

The Portuguese inflicted taxation and forced labor on the African population of Angola, and contracted many to work on the cocoa plantations in São Tomé and Príncipe. Inside Angola, the Portuguese introduced pass laws, similar to those in South Africa. The passes were called cadernata *and Africans were forced to carry them wherever they went. Those accused of crimes were often punished by being beaten on the palms of their hands.*

Construction of the Benguela railroad began in the early part of the century, encouraging the arrival of more white settlers. The economy of Angola grew slowly and all development was directed towards Portugal. The local population was subjected to forced labor and had little stake in the country's fortunes. Armed opposition continued until the 1930s and was often put down with considerable brutality. Portugal spent enormous sums of money keeping large armies in their colonies.

In the early 1930s, when Antonio de Oliviera Salazar came to power, more Portuguese settlers arrived in Angola and economic growth increased, especially after World War II (1939–1945).

In 1951 Angola was made an overseas province of Portugal and plans were made to develop industries and hydroelectric power. The Portuguese stated their intention to create a multi-racial society in Angola, based on equality, but most Africans still suffered repression.

© DIAGRAM

Resistance to colonialism

Atrocity
White officers in the Belgian Congo frequently ordered African soldiers under their command to commit savage acts of punishment against their own people.

Under arrest (above)
Mwene Putu Kasong, king of the Yaka people, was arrested by the authorities in 1905 in the Belgian Congo as part of reprisals against resistance to colonialism.

Africans fought against colonialism in many ways. In some cases, they resisted the arrival of the colonial powers, in others they rebelled against the harsh exploitation of colonialism.

European imperialists destroyed African trading empires and networks, and challenged the sovereignty of existing African kingdoms. Between 1891–1894 the Arab Swahili traders of Tippu Tip's empire fought against the setting up of King Léopold's Congo Free State, which destroyed their trading empire.

In what is now Angola the Ovimbundu were important middlemen in trade between the interior and the coast, and were heavily involved in the rubber trade. The arrival of the Portuguese destroyed their economy and led to the Bailundo War (1902–1903). Widespread famine in 1911 led to a further uprising in 1913.

The Mongo fought European rubber agents in the Congo Free State, while the Luba fought wars of resistance against Belgian colonial rule during the period 1907–1917.

Resistance occurred throughout Central Africa, often continuing well into the 1920s and 1930s. In what is now the Republic of Congo, the Teke fought against the harsh regime and exploitation imposed by French colonialism. The Fang in Equatorial Guinea fought against the Spanish, the Baya carried out armed resistance for many years and, in São Tomé and Príncipe, plantation workers staged periodic revolts against harsh treatment.

Although continuous and widespread, these acts of resistance did not halt colonialism and most were put down harshly. More than three-quarters of the Teke population of the Congo were killed in reprisals. However, they laid the seeds of, and provided inspiration for, the African nationalist and liberation movements that occurred later in the century.

xploiting resources

ing copper

s industry boomed in the
0s and 1930s in the
hern part of Northern
desia, now called
bia. Owned by
e settlers, but
ked by African
ers, most of the
its ended up
seas.

Much of Central Africa, rich in minerals,
including discoveries made in the 1920s,
provided great motivation for European
companies for exploitation, particularly
in the areas formerly known as the
Belgian Congo, French
Equatorial Africa, and
Rhodesia.

e Belgian Congo: 1908–1950s

1908 the Belgian government took over the Congo
ee State and renamed it the Belgian Congo.
nditions for Africans were not as harsh as they had
en under Léopold II, but the Congo was still seen
imarily as a field for European investment. Little was
ne to give Africans a share in government or the
onomy. The Europeans built railways and other
ansport facilities and set up large plantations.
The Congo was rich in mineral resources, including
pper, diamonds, and gold. European investors set up
st mining concerns and, by the end of the 1920s,
ining had outstripped agriculture in importance. While
fricans provided the labor force for the growing
ining industry, the managers were Europeans. Some
ining companies built towns for their African workers
d, from the 1930s, many Africans moved from the
untryside into the urban areas.
Christian missionaries provided medical services and
hatever education Africans received. Virtually no
fricans received a secondary education until the mid-
50s, when two universities were opened. By that time
mands for independence were growing.

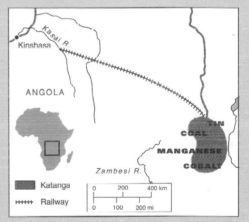

A rich resource
Katanga is an important historical region
of what is now the southern Congo,
formerly known as Zaïre. It was made
part of the Congo Free State, the
personal colony of the Belgian king,
Léopold II, in 1885. Before the arrival of
Europeans, Katangans had been mining
the region's rich mineral deposits. Since
the colonial era, this exploitation
continued, and Katanga became the
most industrialized part of Congo outside
of the capital, Kinshasa.

Central African resistance to European colonialism: 1890–1916

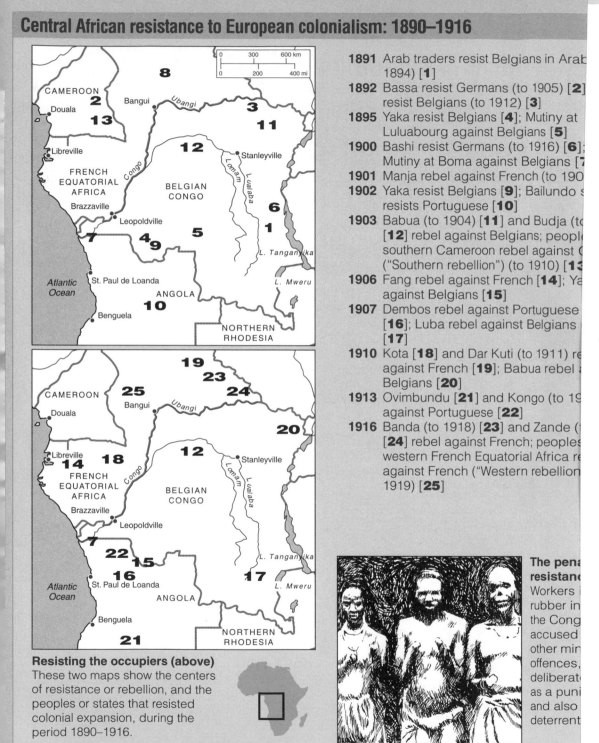

1891 Arab traders resist Belgians in Arab 1894) [1]

1892 Bassa resist Germans (to 1905) [2] resist Belgians (to 1912) [3]

1895 Yaka resist Belgians [4]; Mutiny at Luluabourg against Belgians [5]

1900 Bashi resist Germans (to 1916) [6]; Mutiny at Boma against Belgians [7

1901 Manja rebel against French (to 190

1902 Yaka resist Belgians [9]; Bailundo s resists Portuguese [10]

1903 Babua (to 1904) [11] and Budja (to [12] rebel against Belgians; people southern Cameroon rebel against C ("Southern rebellion") (to 1910) [13

1906 Fang rebel against French [14]; Ya against Belgians [15]

1907 Dembos rebel against Portuguese [16]; Luba rebel against Belgians [17]

1910 Kota [18] and Dar Kuti (to 1911) re against French [19]; Babua rebel a Belgians [20]

1913 Ovimbundu [21] and Kongo (to 19 against Portuguese [22]

1916 Banda (to 1918) [23] and Zande ([24] rebel against French; peoples western French Equatorial Africa re against French ("Western rebellion 1919) [25]

Resisting the occupiers (above)
These two maps show the centers of resistance or rebellion, and the peoples or states that resisted colonial expansion, during the period 1890–1916.

The pena resistan
Workers i rubber in the Cong accused other min offences, deliberate as a puni and also deterrent

French Equatorial Africa: 1910–1950

In 1910 the French combined their Central African colonies – Gabon, Middle Congo, and Oubangi-Shari (now Central African Republic) – into one federation called French Equatorial Africa. A governor-general administered the federation from the capital, Brazzaville, and there was a deputy governor in each territory.

   Until the 1930s, French licensed companies controlled what is now Gabon, using whatever methods they found necessary to exploit the region's resources and people. Forced labor was common practice and there were revolts against the harsh regime.

   From the late 1920s the French developed cotton cultivation in what is now the Central African Republic and improved the infrastructure. Resistance continued until the 1930s. Much of the region was leased to companies, which used harsh methods to exploit both resources and people.

Ruthless exploitation
For the first few decades of the 20th century, cotton, timber, and coffee were the main resources of the area then known as French Equatorial Africa. Methods used to exploit these resources by the French colonial authorities were usually harsh.

Rhodesia: 1900s–1950s

During the early 1900s, European colonists developed copper and lead mining in what was then Northern Rhodesia (now Zambia). In 1909 a railway running from Livingstone to Ndola was completed, and some 1,500 Europeans settled in the region. During the 1920s, extensive copper deposits were discovered in what became known as the "Zambian Copperbelt." Mining was one of the few occupations open to Africans and, by the late 1930s, some 20,000 African laborers were working in the copper mines, which were owned by the white settlers. Profits from the mines went overseas. African workers experienced ill treatment and racial discrimination and were forced to live on "native reserves." They were forbidden to form labor unions, but protested against conditions in a number of strikes between 1935–1956. The copper industry took labor from the rural areas and disrupted whole communities.

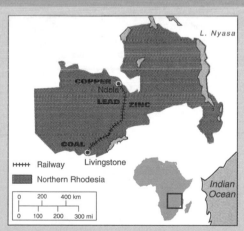

Mining for minerals
Northern Rhodesia (now Zambia) formerly contained areas rich in mineral deposits. In addition to a great deal of copper, lead, zinc, and coal could also be found, mined, and transported by rail.

© DIAGRAM

Central African Federation

1890s British South Africa Company (BSAC) takes over Lozi territory and establishes a colony called Barotseland, later known as Northern Rhodesia

1891 British create colony of Nyasaland
1915 Chilembwe uprising, British Central Africa
1924 British government takes over Northern Rhodesia.
1953 Central African Federation formed. It includes Northern Rhodesia (Zambia), Southern Rhodesia (Zimbabwe), and Nyasaland (Malawi)
1963 CAF dissolved
1964 Northern Rhodesia becomes independent as Zambia

Between 1953 and 1963 the British created a white-minority ruled federation called the Central African Federation (CAF). It consisted of the colonies of Northern Rhodesia (now Zambia), Southern Rhodesia (now Zimbabwe), and Nyasaland (now Malawi).

The British arrived in what is now Zambia in the mid-19th century. In the 1890s, agents of Cecil Rhodes' British South Africa Company (BSAC) signed a treaty with Lewinaka, the Lozi king, which gave them control of the Lozi lands. The BSAC, which colonized much of central-south Africa, turned the Lozi kingdom into a colony called Barotseland, which remained under British control until the 1960s.

The Company promised to make an annual payment of £2,000 to Lewinaka and help in setting up schools, hospitals, industries, and postal and transport systems. In exchange, the Company was granted absolute and exclusive rights over all trade. In actuality, the BSAC invested nothing, and education was left to Christian missionaries. Lewinaka received some payments, supplemented by taxes, and there were some transport developments. By 1907 his power had declined and the region had become largely a source of cheap labor for Company enterprises elsewhere in central and southern Africa.

In 1924 the British government took over Barotesland from the BSAC and it became known as Northern Rhodesia. White settlers arrived in the region, and Africans were moved onto "reserves."

Central African Protectorate

The colony of Nyasaland was created by the British in 1891 in an attempt to halt both Portuguese and German colonial influence in the area. It became the Central African Protectorate in 1893, but reverted to the name of Nyasaland in 1907. This map shows the situation in 1892.

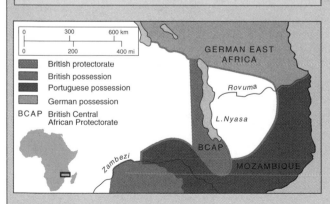

British protectorate
British possession
Portuguese possession
German possession
BCAP British Central African Protectorate

In 1891 the British, to halt Portuguese colonial influence, created a colony called Nyasaland (now known as Malawi). It became the Central African Protectorate in 1893, but reverted to Nyasaland in 1907. Under colonial rule, there was some economic development, including road and rail construction, and also the introduction of cash crops, but the local population remained poor.

In 1953, despite African opposition, Nyasaland was joined with Northern Rhodesia (Zambia) and Southern Rhodesia (Zimbabwe) to form a new political unit: the Central African Federation of Rhodesia and Nyasaland. Political power lay in the hands of the white minority who ruled the federation. Britain continued to control Nyasaland and Northern Rhodesia but some power went to a federal government based in white-dominated

Salisbury (now Harare) in Southern Rhodesia.

Black nationalists in all three territories opposed the federation. In Malawi, the black nationalist Dr Hastings Banda spearheaded opposition; in Northern Rhodesia, the Northern Rhodesia African Congress (formed 1948) under Harry Nkumbula fought strenuously against the federation. From 1959 Kenneth Kaunda and the United National Independence Party (UNIP) led the fight against ongoing colonial rule.

In 1963 the Federation was dissolved and, in 1964, Northern Rhodesia gained independence as Zambia.

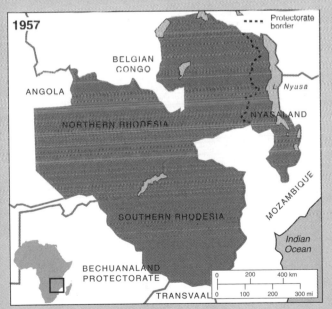

Central African Federation
The British colonies of Southern Rhodesia, Northern Rhodesia, and Nyasaland were joined in 1953 to form the Central African Federation. In the face of continuing opposition from black nationalists, it was dissolved in 1963. This map shows the situation in 1957.

Dr Hastings Banda
He became the prime minister of Malawi (formerly known as Nyasaland) in 1963, president in 1966, and "president for life" in 1971. He is shown here in a typical pose, sporting a fly-whisk which he used to discourage any petitioners he met while touring around the country.

© DIAGRAM

Joseph Kasavubu
Leader of the ABAKO nationalist party, he became the first president, in 1960, of the Democratic Republic of Congo. He was subsequently deposed in 1965 by General Mobutu Sese Seko.

Victory!
This stamp marks the eventual supremacy, in 1975, of the MPLA against the Portuguese dictatorship in Angola.

Liberation and independence

In 1960 colonial rule in Africa came to a rapid end. In what British Prime Minister Harold Macmillan described as a "wind of change" all the Central African countries achieved independence between 1960–75. In some cases, independence was achieved relatively peacefully, in others, such as Angola, independence followed bitter liberation struggles.

French Equatorial Africa
During World War II (1939–1945), the Free French forces had made the Congo, particularly Brazzaville, a base for struggles against the Germans and the Vichy regime.

After the war, demands mounted for independence and, in 1946, Oubangi-Shari, Gabon, and Middle Congo became French overseas territories. General Charles de Gaulle became a hero when he granted internal self-government in 1958, and independence in 1960.

Belgian Congo
In the Belgian Congo, the Belgian government had planned for gradual self-government. However, Congo nationalists, notably Joseph Kasavubu, leader of the ABAKO party, and Patrice Lumumba, leader of the leftist *Mouvement National Congolais,* became increasingly active. In 1959 nationalist riots broke out in Kinshasa, and the Belgians lost control.

A conference took place in Brussels in Jan–Feb 1960, which included Congolese nationalists and, in June, the colony became independent as the Democratic Republic of the Congo, with Lumumba as prime minister.

Angola
In 1951 Angola became an overseas province of Portugal but nationalist opposition mounted. In 1961, inspired by liberation movements elsewhere, Angolans rose in revolt. The *Movimento Popular de Libertação de Angola* (MPLA), which had been founded in 1956 and had support from the Mbundu people, staged a revolt in Luanda. The Portuguese army quashed the revolt, and many Angolans fled to the Congo.

The liberation war continued with two other groups joining the struggle. In 1962 a group of refugees, led by

Holden Roberto, organized the *Frente Nacional de Libertação de Angola* (FNLA). The FNLA, which maintained supply and training bases in the Congo, waged war in northern Angola.

From 1966 a third rival group, the *União Nacional para a Indepêndencia Total de Angola* (UNITA), under Jonas Savimbi, supported by the Ovimbundu, fought in the south. By the 1970s Portugal had more than 50,000 troops in Angola fighting guerrillas.

In 1972 the heads of the FNLA and MPLA assumed joint leadership of a newly-formed Supreme Council for the Liberation of Angola. In 1974 a coup in Portugal overthrew the Portuguese dictatorship, and the new government negotiated independence for Angola, which was achieved in 1975. The MPLA formed the first government.

A sign of the times
A 1970s poster reflects the continuing and bitter struggle for independence in Angola.

São Tomé and Príncipe

During the 1960s nationalists, including Manuel Pinto Da Costa and Miguel Trovoada, set up the Movement for the Liberation of São Tomé and Príncipe (MLSTP). In 1970 Portugal introduced some reforms but opposition continued.

In 1972 the OAU recognized the MLSTP and, following the coup in Portugal in 1974, the islands finally gained their independence, in 1975.

Keeping the peace (right)
A Swedish soldier takes action to avoid a civil disturbance in the Congo in 1959. The soldier wears the flag of the United Nations on his uniform; it comprises a map of the world surrounded by a wreath of olive branches which symbolizes peace.

© DIAGRAM

WARS, COUPS, AND DICTATORSHIPS

REPUBLIQUE CENTRAFRICAINE
30

JEAN BEDEL BOKASSA

Following independence, the political situation in Central African countries was unstable. Country borders had been created by the European powers when they colonized the region, and they did not take account of ethnic rivalries, which emerged after independence, causing conflict. This happened, for instance, in the Democratic Republic of the Congo (formerly the Belgian Congo), which was almost immediately plunged into a civil war. Angola too went into a long and damaging civil war as the different liberation and ethnic groups fought against each other, backed by foreign powers.

The political and economic systems of the newly independent countries were also fragile. There had been little time to put democratic systems in place, and many of the Central African nations, such as the Central African Republic, experienced military *coups d'état* and political takeovers, which enabled dictators, such as Emperor Bokassa, to assume absolute power.

Birth of an empire (left)
When Jean Bédel Bokassa declared himself as "emperor" in 1976, he renamed the Central African Republic as the "Central African Empire."

Central Africa: a history of strife, 1960–1974

1960–1975	Central African nations achieve independence
1960–1963	Katanga secedes and is reunited
1961	Patrice Lumumba is murdered
1962	Central African Republic (CAR) becomes a one-party state
1963	Government is overthrown, Republic of Congo
1964	Military coup, Gabon
1964	Kenneth Kaunda becomes president of Zambia
1965	Military coup, Dem. Rep. of Congo: Joseph–Désiré Mobutu takes power
1966	Military coup, CAR: Bokassa seizes power
1968	Gabon becomes one-party state under Omar Bongo
1969	Military coup, Congo Republic: Marien Ngouabi seizes power
1970	Congo Republic declared Marxist country
1970	Mobutu sets up one-party state, Dem. Rep. of Congo
1970	One-party dictatorship set up under Macías Nguema, Equatorial Guinea
1971–1997	Dem. Rep. of Congo renamed Zaïre.
1972	Bokassa becomes president for life, CAR
1972	Zambia becomes one-party state; UNIP only legal party
1974	Civil war breaks out between MPLA, FNLA and UNITA, Angola

As dictators became more powerful, they increasingly controlled all aspects of life, often putting their own interests above those of the country and causing hardship and economic problems for the local population. Intervention and interference by non-Central African countries, including the two superpowers of the USA and the Soviet Union, who wanted to increase their influence in the region, often made matters worse.

As a result Central Africa suffered years of political and social turmoil after 1960. By the early 1990s Central African countries were moving towards democracy even if there were difficulties. However, war and its devastating effects continued to dominate Angola and the Democratic Republic of Congo well into the 21st century.

Frederick Chiluba (above)
He defeated Kenneth Kaunda in multiparty elections in 1991, thus becoming the second president of Zambia. He was reelected again in 1996, but stood down in 2001

Moise Tshombe (above)
He was the prime minister of Katanga province in the former Belgian Congo which became independent as the Democratic Republic of Congo, on June 30, 1960.

Central Africa: a history of strife, 1974–2002

1975	MPLA forms government; newly-independent Angola
1976	Bokassa declares Central African Empire
1977–1978	Rebellions in Shaba (formerly Katanga) province
1977	Ngouabi assassinated, Congo Republic
1979	French-backed military coup overthrows Bokassa, CAR
1979	Military coup, Equatorial Guinea: Mbasango seizes power
1980s	Civil war, Angola; MPLA and UNITA agree ceasefire 1989
1986	Rioting in Zambia
1987	Bokassa imprisoned, CAR
1988	Socialist policies modified, São Tomé and Príncipe
1990	Opposition parties legalized, Gabon; multiparty elections held, São Tomé and Príncipe
1991	Multiparty elections, Zambia
1992–2002	Intermittent civil war, Angola
1992	Multiparty constitutions set up in CAR, Rep. of Congo, and Equatorial Guinea
1996	Hutu-Tutsi conflict spreads to Dem. Rep. of Congo
1997	Mobutu overthrown, Laurent Kabila becomes president, Dem. Rep. of Congo
1998	Civil war breaks out again in Dem. Rep. of Congo
2002	Ceasefire, Angola; fighting continues in eastern Dem. Rep. of Congo

© DIAGRAM

Civil War in Angola

A supporter of the MPLA

This young soldier belonged to the Popular Movement for the Liberation of Angola. The MPLA opposed UNITA and the FNLA during the struggle for independence in Angola during the 1960s.

After independence Angola experienced more then 25 years of almost continuous civil war. During the 1960s three main liberation groups fought for independence: Holden Roberto's Front for the Liberation of Angola (FNLA), the Marxist-influenced Popular Movement for the Liberation of Angola (MPLA), and the National Union for the Total Liberation of Angola (UNITA), led by Jonas Savimbi.

Angola became independent in 1975 with the MPLA forming the government. However, rivalry between the three groups meant that civil war raged on, exacerbated by intervention from outside countries. The Soviet Union and Cuba backed the MPLA who, by 1976, had gained control over most of Angola. The FNLA became less important in the early 1980s but UNITA rebels in the south of the country continued fighting the MPLA, backed by South Africa which was mounting its own campaign against the Southwest Africa People's Organization (SWAPO), a Namibian liberation group based in Angola.

In the late 1980s the United States provided aid to UNITA and demanded the withdrawal of Cuban troops and an end to Soviet assistance. Agreement was reached in 1988 and Cuban troops began to withdraw.

In 1991 the ruling MPLA and UNITA agreed a ceasefire, and the government, under President dos

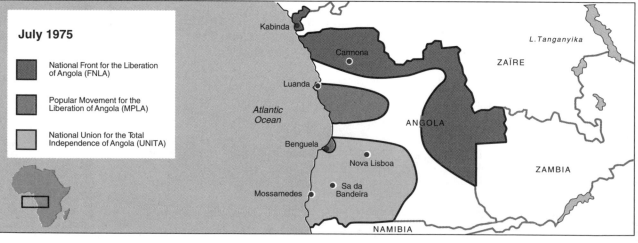

July 1975

- National Front for the Liberation of Angola (FNLA)
- Popular Movement for the Liberation of Angola (MPLA)
- National Union for the Total Independence of Angola (UNITA)

Santos, agreed to make Angola a multiparty state. In 1992 the MPLA, which had renounced its Marxist policies, won the elections and dos Santos was reelected president. UNITA refused to accept the result, making allegations of fraud. In 1992 bitter fighting broke out between rebel UNITA troops and government forces, which caused great damage to the country. Although UNITA made initial victories, the MPLA eventually gained the upper hand.

In 1994, dos Santos and Savimbi signed the Lusaka Protocol to end the conflict. It was agreed that UNITA troops would be integrated into the government's armed forces and that demobilization would begin. United Nations (UN) peacekeeping forces arrived in 1995. In 1997 a coalition government was formed, including UNITA deputies. Savimbi was offered the vice-presidency but refused.

In 1999 full-scale civil war broke out once more. Funded by oil revenues, the government refused further talks with Savimbi, whose UNITA weaponry was funded by diamond smuggling. Savimbi died in battle in February 2002. A ceasefire was signed in April 2002.

By 2002 thousands of people had died as a result of war and some 4 million had been displaced. The country was also facing a severe food crisis with widespread famine and at least 1 million people were starving.

Liberation group
These soldiers belonged to the National Union for the Total Liberation of Angola. They opposed the FNLA and the MPLA during the struggle for independence in Angola in the 1960s.

A 27-year struggle (below)
The civil war in Angola lasted from 1975 until a ceasefire was signed in 2002. The map (opposite) shows the situation in July 1975, when the MPLA gained contol of the Angolan capital, Luanda; the map (below) shows the situation in February 1976, when the MPLA government assumed power.

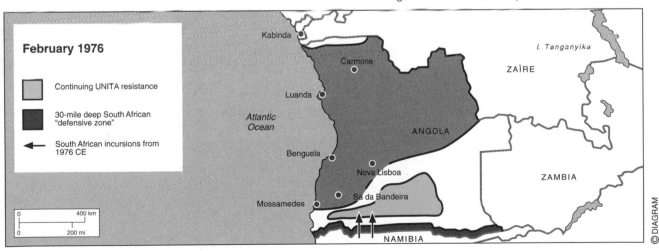

February 1976

- Continuing UNITA resistance
- 30-mile deep South African "defensive zone"
- ← South African incursions from 1976 CE

Kabinda
Carmona
Luanda
Atlantic Ocean
Benguela
Nova Lisboa
Mossamedes
Sa da Bandeira
NAMIBIA
ANGOLA
ZAÏRE
L. Tanganyika
ZAMBIA

0 — 400 km
0 — 200 mi

©DIAGRAM

War in The Congo

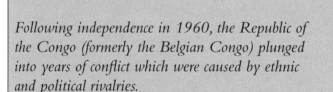

Children at war
Strife in the Congo, which resulted in freedom for the former Belgian colony, involved children as well as adults.

Following independence in 1960, the Republic of the Congo (formerly the Belgian Congo) plunged into years of conflict which were caused by ethnic and political rivalries.

Katanga seccession

Following elections, Joseph Kasavubu, a member of the Bakongo political party, became president, with Patrice Lumumba, who had played a leading role in the liberation movement, as prime minister. The two were political opponents who agreed to share power.

Almost immediately, Moise Tshombe, provisional head of mineral-rich Katanga province, declared the province an independent state. Belgian nationals living in the Congo were attacked and Belgium sent troops to the country to protect its citizens and mining interests. The UN Security Council voted to send a peacekeeping force to the area. Lumumba turned to the Soviet Union for help but was dismissed by Kasavubu. He was subsequently arrested and murdered.

By the end of 1960, Congo was a divided country. General Mobutu held the west, including Léopoldville, Gizenga, self-styled successor to Lumumba, controlled the east, Albert Kalonji controlled the Luba state of South Kasai, which had broken away, and Tshombe headed Katanga, backed by Belgian and other foreign soldiers.

In 1961 Tshombe was arrested but subsequently released. UN forces began disarming Katangese soldiers but war broke out again when Tshombe pushed once more for independence. By 1963, however, Tshombe was forced to back down, the country was reunited and UN forces withdrew from the conflict.

40 years of conflict in Central Africa

1960 Congo becomes an independent republic
1960–1963 Katanga province secedes and is reunited
1961 Patrice Lumumba is murdered
1964 Widespread rebellion; white mercenaries arrive
1965 Joseph-Desiré Mobutu becomes president
1970 Mobutu declares a one-party state
1971–1979 Congo renamed Zaïre as part of "authenticity" measures
1973 Foreign-owned businesses seized
1976 International Monetary Fund (IMP) backs economic stabilization plan
1977–1978 French help to suppress two rebellions in Shaba (Katanga) province
1984 Mobutu is re-elected president; he is the only candidate
1986 CIA uses Zaïre as base to supply arms to UNITA rebels in Angola
1990 Mobutu lifts bans on political parties
1991 Economic problems cause widespread rioting
1994 One million Hutu refugees arrive in Zaïre from Rwanda
1996 Hutu-Tutsi conflict (Rwanda and Burundi) spreads to Tutsi in eastern Zaïre. Rwandan army invades to topple Mobutu
1997 Coup: Tutsi-backed Laurent Kabila overthrows Mobutu. Country renamed Democratic Republic of Congo; Shaba is renamed Katanga
1998 Civil war breaks out: Angola; Chad and others support Kabila; Burundi, Rwanda, and Uganda support rebels
2001 Kabila assassinated. His son, Joseph, becomes president

Provincial revolts
Following the withdrawal of Belgian troops in 1960 from the Congo, a series of revolts occurred which the government in power, aided by UN forces, attempted to bring under their control. Casualties were inevitable.

In 1964 Tshombe became prime minister, a move which caused widespread rebellions. White mercenaries arrived in the country and, with US help and Belgian troops, the central government gradually regained control although political rivalries continued.

In 1965 the army seized power under General Joseph Desiré Mobutu, who declared himself president. Rebellions occurred in 1966 and 1967.

In 1970 Mobutu made the country a one-party state, heading the only political party – the Popular Movement of the Revolution (PMR).

Crisis in the Congo (right)

This map shows the area of Katanga secession from 1960–1963, and the maximum area of rebel advance in 1964, during the unrest which took place in the Congo during the period 1960–1965.

Maximum area of rebel advances

Maximum area of Katanga secession

| 0 | 300 | 600 km |
| 0 | 200 | 400 mi |

CENTRAL AFRICAN REPUBLIC

CONGO

Atlantic Ocean

Brazzaville

Léopoldville

ANGOLA

L Tanganyika

© DIAGRAM

A formula for disaster

In 1971 Mobutu introduced a policy of so-called African authenticity, renaming the Democratic Republic of Congo as Zaïre, and its capital as Kinshasa. He also changed his own name to Mobutu Sese Seko. He banned Christian teaching, closed Christian schools and followed increasingly repressive policies. He also became rich at his country's expense. It was the height of the Cold War and Western powers, seeing his rule as a buffer against Communism, tended to ignore the corruption in the country.

Mobutu centralized the administration and, in 1973, nationalized many foreign-owned firms in an attempt to reduce unemployment. In 1974 he forced European investors out of the country but, later, unsuccessfully invited them back. The country went into economic decline and Mobutu faced increasing political opposition and pressure to restore democracy. His policy of giving members of his own ethnic group, the Ngbanda, control over security matters led to conflict and there were attempted coups during 1975–1978. Opposition political parties grew, one of which, the National Liberation Front of Congo (FNLC), working from Angola, launched a rebellion. It was put down after French, Belgian, and Moroccan troops intervened.

In the early 1980s, opposition groups organized in exile in the hope of overthrowing Mobutu. In 1989 the country defaulted on a loan from Belgium and development programs were cancelled. In 1990 Mobutu ended single-party rule. He appointed a transitional government but postponed elections.

Mobutu Sese Seko
He served as president from 1965–1997, when he fled the country accused of corruption. Ruling in a dictatorial manner, he held the country together despite the efforts of ethnic groups threatening to pull it apart.

Portrait of a despot: ten key stages

- Deposed first president in 1965
- Created one-party state
- Banned Christian schools
- Aquired personal wealth at the expense of his country
- Centralized administration
- Nationalized foreign-owned firms placed securely in the hands of one ethnic group (his own) in 1973
- Forced European investors out of the country in 1974
- United foreign troops to suppress uprisings
- Defaulted on foreign loan from Belgium in 1989
- Fled the country in 1997

The conflict spreads

In 1994 conditions worsened when more than a million Hutu refugees took refuge in eastern Zaïre, fleeing the conflict in Rwanda. Ethnic fighting between Hutu and Tutsi spilled over into Zaïre. Supported by Uganda and Rwanda, and with aid from Zambia and Angola, Laurent Kabila, led Tutsi rebels in Zaïre in a rebellion against Mobutu. His Alliance of Democratic Forces for the Liberation of Congo-Zaïre advanced westward. In 1997 Mobutu fled the country and Kabila became president, renaming Zaïre the Democratic Republic of Congo.

Kabila promised elections but his regime became increasingly repressive. He failed to revive the economy or prevent attacks upon Congolese Tutsi by Hutu in the mid-1990s. In 1998 a group of ethnic Tutsi Congolese forces, supported by Rwanda, Uganda, and Burundi, rebelled against Kabila's rule and began advancing on Kinshasa. Angola, Chad, Namibia, and Zimbabwe sent troops to help Kabila's government, creating a major conflict.

In 1999, following a peace conference in Lusaka, Zambia, six African heads of state, including Laurent Kabila, and representatives of rebel factions signed a peace agreement but it failed to stop the fighting. In 2001 Kabila was assassinated. His son, Joseph, succeeded him and lifted the existing ban on political parties.

Peace talks began again but by 2002 there was still bitter fighting in eastern Congo. According to an American aid agency, fighting in eastern Congo alone had caused an estimated 2.5 million deaths.

Results of the tyranny: ten key facts

- Millions of displaced persons
- Constant threat of starvation
- No education for majority of people
- No effective health care
- No civil liberties
- No reliable sources of income
- Ethnic conflict spilling over borders with neighboring states
- Escalating civil war within the country
- Political instability continues well into new millennium
- 2.5 million deaths estimated as a result of fighting in eastern Congo alone to date

Another victim
Shabunda, situated in the eastern Democratic Republic of Congo, was the center of renewed conflict in July 2002. This man waits to see the only doctor in what remains of the local hospital

© DIAGRAM

83

Former French colonies

The Central African Republic, the Republic of Congo, and Gabon all achieved independence from France in 1960. Over the following years, each of these three nations suffered a variety of political problems and conflict.

Central African Republic

This became a one-party state in 1962 under David Dacko. Corruption was widespread and the economy stagnated. In 1966 a military coup d'état brought General Jean Bédel Bokassa to power. In 1972 he made himself president for life.

Bokassa's regime was particularly harsh and the ruling elite were corrupt. In 1981 a military coup brought General André Kolingba to power. Strikes and demonstrations mounted and, in 1992, the country adopted a multiparty constitution.

In 1993 Ange-Félix Patassé was elected president. The country was facing bankruptcy. Teachers, civil servants, and soldiers had not received wages and in 1996 the army mutinied. French troops arrived and Patassé agreed to form a new government. Despite this, fighting broke out again in 1997. A UN peacekeeping force replaced French troops but the country was still in an uneasy situation in 2002.

Republic of Congo

The first president, Abbé Fulbert Youlou, was overthrown in 1963. The new president, Alphonse Massamba-Débat, adopted a one-party system and socialist policies, taking over and expanding state-run

1960–1970	1971–1980

Congo Republic

1960 Aug. 15 Congo becomes an independent republic; Fulbert Youlou becomes first president
1963 Labor uprising overturns the Youlou government
1964 Congo becomes a one-party state
1969 A group of army officers, under control of Capt. Marien Ngouabi, seizes power

1970 Congo declares itself a Marxist country and is renamed People's Republic of Congo
1972 President Ngouabi defeats an attempted coup
1977 Ngouabi is assassinated; Col. Jaochim Yhombi-Opango succeeds
1979 Yhombi-Opango resigns; Col. Denis Sassou-Nguesso becomes president

Central African Republic

1960 Aug. 13 Oubangi-Shari becomes independent as CAR; David Dacko becomes first president
1962 Dacko makes the country a one party state
1966 Gen. Jean-Bédel Bokassa seizes power in a military coup

1972 Bokassa becomes president for life
1976 Bokassa appoints himself emperor, and renames CAR the Central African Empire
1979 Bokassa is overthrown by a French-supported coup

Gabon

1960 Aug. 17 Gabon becomes independent; Léon M'Ba is first president
1964 Attempt to overthrow M'Ba is crushed by French troops
1967 M'Ba dies in office; he is succeeded by Bernard-Albert Bongo
1968 Bongo declares Gabon a one-party state

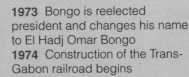

1973 Bongo is reelected president and changes his name to El Hadj Omar Bongo
1974 Construction of the Trans-Gabon railroad begins
1975 Gabon becomes a member of OPEC
1979 Bongo is reelected president in elections in which he is the only candidate

farming and industry. In 1969 the army, under Marien Ngouabi, seized power. He was assassinated in 1977, and a military council took over, appointing Joachim Yhombi-Opango president. He was ousted and, in 1979, Denis Sassou-Nguesso became head of state.

In 1990 Congo abandoned its Communist policies and, in 1992, democracy was restored when the first free elections were held. Pascal Lissouba was elected president. Ethnic and political rivalries, as well as government attempts to disarm local militia, who supported Sasso-Nguesso, led to conflict.

In 1997 Sasso-Nguesso's forces, supported by Angola, seized Brazzaville. Lissouba fled into exile. Between 10,000 and 15,000 people died in the fighting and the country's economy was seriously damaged. Sasso-Nguesso became president and a peace agreement was signed in 1999.

Gabon

The first president was Léon M'Ba, a Fang, who had led the liberation struggle. He died in 1967 and was succeeded by Omar Bongo, a Muslim convert, who made Gabon a one-party state. His rule was authoritarian and conservative, but he attracted foreign investment and Gabon's economy flourished. Political opposition mounted, stimulated by economic problems.

In 1990 Bongo's government legalized political parties. Despite allegations of fraud, Bongo and the PDG continued to win elections.

1981–1990

1988 Conference in Brazzaville paves the way for Namibia's independence

1987 Bokassa is imprisoned for murder and embezzlement

1982 National Reorientation Movement is suppressed
1984 Bongo gives France permission to build a nuclear plant in Gabon
1986 Bongo is again reelected president in elections in which he is the only candidate
1989 Riots follow the murder of Joseph Redjambe, the leader of the Gabonese Progressive Party, in Libreville

1991–2002

1990 Congo renounces Marxism
1991 Political parties are legalized
1992 A new multiparty constitution is approved by a referendum
1993 President Sassou-Nguesso is defeated in elections by Lissouba
1997 Sassou-Nguesso seizes power with the support of Angolan troops

1992 Multiparty constitution introduced
1993 Ange-Félix Patassé becomes president after multiparty elections
1996 France helps suppress rebellion
1997 President Patassé calls for the withdrawal of French troops amid growing anti-French hostility
1999 Patassé is reelected president, defeating Kolingba

1990 Opposition parties are legalized; the ruling Gabonese Democratic Party wins the assembly elections
1993 Bongo retains the presidency after he wins Gabon's first multiparty elections
1996 Gabon withdraws from OPEC
1998 Bongo wins presidential elections with 66 percent of the vote

Equatorial Guinea after occupation

A wasted resource
Revenue from oil seldom reached the national treasury after its discovery in 1992, although the economy did show some signs of improvement.

Francisco Macías Nguema
The first president of Equatorial Guinea between 1968–1979, he was a brutal dictator who launched a reign of terror, and ordered numerous political murders. Nguema was eventually overthrown in a military coup led by his nephew, tried, and executed.

One of Africa's smallest nations, Equatorial Guinea gained independence from Spain in 1968, but democracy was short-lived. The country's first president was Francisco Macías Nguema, a Fang from Rio Muni, and a member of the Esangui clan. In 1970 Nguema made the country a one-party state, merging all political parties into the United National Party (PUN), which he headed. In 1971, he declared himself president for life.

Nguema's rule was tyrannical and, until he was deposed in 1979, he headed a reign of terror. Campaigns were carried out against intellectuals, and anyone accused of plotting to overthrow his regime was killed or imprisoned. It is estimated that some 25,000 to 80,000 inhabitants of the country were killed by the government, and many thousands fled, including a large number of skilled and educated people.

Nigerian workers, who had been brought into the country, and who demanded higher wages, were also brutally suppressed, causing tension between Nigeria and Equatorial Guinea. In 1975 schools were closed and, in 1977, Nguema broke off relations with Spain. Foreign

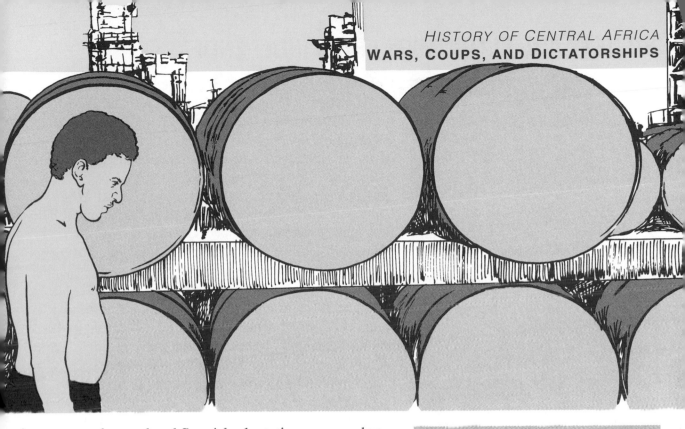

investment dropped and Spanish plantation owners shut down operations, causing severe economic problems.

In 1979 the army staged a coup, executing Nguema and installing his nephew, Obiang Nguema Mbasogo as head of state. He lifted restrictions on the Roman Catholic Church, freed 5,000 political prisoners, and restored diplomatic relations with Spain and the United States. He restored some democracy but the military council remained the sole political body. Economic reforms, including joining the Franc Zone, helped to stabilize the economy of the nation.

Despite reforms, Obiang Nguema maintained control. Attempted coups were put down harshly, and the government was accused of human rights abuses. In 1992 laws were passed providing for a multiparty democracy. Elections took place in 1993, but only one party, Obiang Nguema's Democratic Party for Equatorial Guinea (PDGE), gained significant power. Most opponents had boycotted the elections.

In the 1996 and 2002 elections, Nguema won landslide victories amid accusations of fraud and intimidation.

São Tomé and Príncipe

The first president was Manuel Pinto da Costa, with Miguel Trovoada as prime minister. Both had been

involved in the liberation struggle. The new government adopted socialist policies, and made the Movement for the Liberation of São Tomé and Príncipe (MLSTP) the only legal political party. A secret police force was established to maintain control.

During the 1970s there were splits in the MLSTP, and plots against da Costa. Trovoada was removed, imprisoned and went into exile. Da Costa modified his socialist policies and, in 1991, the first free elections took place. Trovoada, back from exile, was elected as leader of a new party – the Democratic Convergence. The secret police were abolished.

In 1995 the island of Príncipe was granted self-rule.

© DIAGRAM

SOCIETY AND ECONOMICS AFTER INDEPENDENCE

CEEAC
Established in 1982, the Economic Community of Central African States, which comprises 11 members, aims to promote regional economic cooperation, and to establish a Central African Common Market.

LOMÉ Convention
Signed in 1975, this trade agreement, concluded between 46 developing countries from Africa, the Caribbean and the Pacific countries, aims to maintain links between the European Community and its former colonies in respect of trade and development finance.

ECA
Established in 1982, the Economic Commission for Africa is mandated by the UN to support the economic and social development of its 53 member states, foster regional integration, and promote Africa's development.

OAU
Established in 1963, the Organization of African Unity was wound up in July 2002 and replaced by the African Union (AU).

AU
Established in July 2002, the African Union was founded to promote economic growth, development, better government, and self-sufficiency in Africa.

ADB
Established in 1964, the African Development Bank is dedicated to the fight against poverty, and improving the lives of people in Africa.

UDEAC
Established in 1964, the Central African Customs and Economic Union promotes the establishment of a Central African Common Market. It has six members, and is now better known as the Monetary and Economic Community of Central Africa (CEMAC).

Colonial rule had a destructive effect on the economies and societies of Central Africa. Colonial rulers disrupted the economies of the region, put in licensed agents, and concentrated on extracting minerals and other resources. Most had little interest in developing resources for the indigenous African populations.

After independence, the countries of Central Africa attempted to build up their societies and economies. The immediate economic prospects were poor and wars, political instability, and dictatorships prevented or damaged economic growth. For example, in Angola, the long civil war drained the country's finances and damaged its infrastructure. Fighting damaged the Benguela railroad, which had played a vital role in the country's economy by transporting minerals for worldwide export. Revenues from offshore oil, discovered in the 1990s, were diverted to fund the ongoing conflict.

During the 1970s, brutal dictatorships in Equatorial Guinea and the Central African Republic left their countries' economies unstable and weakened. The effects caused great hardship to their people, and there was little opportunity to plow money back into social needs, such as health and education.

To some extent, Gabon was an exception. Political dictatorship there brought some stability and economic success. Private enterprise attracted foreign investment, which helped the country to build up its rich mineral resources, making it one of Africa's most successful economies. Revenues from oil enabled substantial investment in health services which, by the early 1990s, were among the best in Africa. Even so, most of Gabon's people remained very poor.

Pan-African organizations
These were founded in an attempt to create structures that would avoid clashes between different nations in Africa, and also to allow them to gain strength from acting in unison.

Developing economies

1957	Oil discovered in the Congo
1970	Zambian government acquires controlling interest in copper-mining industry
1973	Government nationalizes foreign businesses, Zaïre (Dem. Rep. of Congo)
1973– 1975	Railroad built, with Chinese aid, from Copperbelt, Zambia, to Dar es Salaam (Tanzania)
1975– 1996	Gabon belongs to Organization of Petroleum-Exporting Countries (OPEC)
1976	International Monetary Fund (IMF) supports economic stabilization plan for Zaïre (Dem. Rep. of Congo)
1983– 1984	Drought hits São Tomé and Príncipe
1984	France allowed to build nuclear power station in Gabon but plans abandoned in 1986 after Chornobyl disaster in Russia
1985	Equatorial Guinea adopts African Franc Zone currency
1986	Zambian government introduces austerity measures; leads to widespread rioting
1988	IMF provides reform package for São Tomé and Príncipe
1990– 1995	Central African countries adopt multiparty constitutions
1991	Engineers begin rebuilding Benguela railroad, Angola, after destruction caused by civil war
1994	Currency devalued: Congo Republic, Democratic Republic of Congo, Equatorial Guinea, and Gabon suffer economic hardship and social unrest
1995	Outbreak of Ebola virus in Democratic Republic of Congo
1996	Angola and São Tomé and Príncipe join Community of Portuguese-speaking countries
2003	Chad's oil revenues expected to reach US$80–140 million

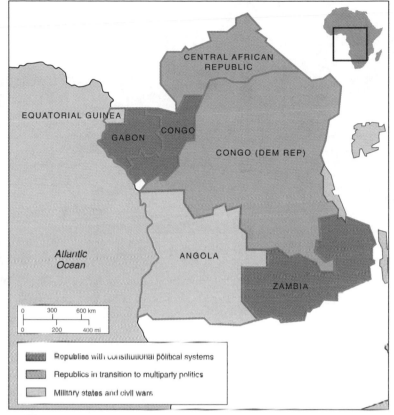

Key:
- Republics with constitutional political systems
- Republics in transition to multiparty politics
- Military states and civil wars

Political systems (above)
By the early 2000s, two multiparty systems operated in 13 African nations, while 21 were republics with constitutional political systems (i.e. they have presidents and an agreed electoral system). Military regimes were in control in 12 countries.

Devaluation (right)
A man from the Central African Federation carries bundles of francs devalued by 50 percent in 1994 as a result of pressure from the International Monetary Fund (IMF) and France.

© DIAGRAM

89

Mining and industry

Mufulira copper mine (above)
With two other Zambian copper mines, Mufulira went on strike in 1935. However, effective unity between African mineworkers was slow to come in Central Africa.

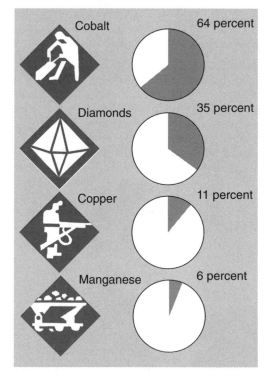

Cobalt — 64 percent

Diamonds — 35 percent

Copper — 11 percent

Manganese — 6 percent

Mineral resources (above)
In the 1980s the region of Central Africa produced the proportions of the world output of cobalt, diamonds, copper, and manganese shown above.

Central Africa is rich in mineral resources. After independence, most economic programs were aimed at exploiting petroleum and other mineral resources, such as copper, diamonds, iron ore, and manganese. However, the population of Central Africa grew rapidly after independence. Emphasis on exploiting minerals diverted resources from producing food for the fast growing population, resulting in widespread poverty, which governments were unable to control.

The emphasis on exporting raw materials also meant that countries were vulnerable to changes in world markets and prices. During the 1970s there was an oil crisis and worldwide recession, causing a sharp fall in the price of oil, copper, and other raw materials. This had a damaging effect on many economies including those of Gabon and the Democratic Republic of the Congo, whose economy virtually collapsed when copper prices fell.

During the 1980s, economies in Central Africa were slow to develop. Following the economic crises of the 1970s, some Central African countries tried to diversify their economies and develop other sources of income. Countries, such as Gabon and the Democratic Republic of the Congo, began to set up manufacturing and processing industries. Within the Congo, engineers used the hydroelectric power of the Congo River to maintain industrial complexes that had first been developed during the colonial era. In 1986 the Trans-Gabon railroad was completed, which linked the new deepwater port of Owendo, near Libreville, with iron ore and manganese deposits at the mining complex at Massoukou. It also opened up one of the last great rainforests to commercial exploitation. In 1983, a hydroelectric station was built in Equatorial Guinea with Chinese assistance. Roads and other communication systems, however, remained very undeveloped.

Franc zone

During the 1980s Equatorial Guinea, Gabon, Congo, and the Central African Republic joined what is known as the African franc zone. To try and introduce some economic stability to their countries, their currencies were linked to the French franc at a fixed rate.

However, they suffered economic hardship when the currency was devalued in 1994 by 50 percent following pressure from the International Monetary Fund (IMF), and from France itself.

Soil degradation (above)
Open-cast copper mines of the kind shown above severely degrade the local environment for decades.

Wealth from oil (below)
Central African oil-related Industries are based around towns and cities, particularly Brazzaville in the Congo.

Using and abusing the land

Selective logging (above)
Commercial loggers now only fell trees they want rather than cutting down and burning all the other trees in the area with a destructive effect on the local ecosystem.

Deforestation (below)
Dead stumps and roots are all that remain once a forest has been completely cleared of trees. Once the roots rot, the soil – which is no longer bound together – washes away. A further impact is the loss of plants and animals that lived within this habitat.

Despite developments in mining and industry, most people continue to rely on farming. Soils in Central Africa easily support subsistence farming, in which a farming family grows and harvests enough for their needs only. Even though occupations became increasingly diverse, up to 80 percent of the population remained linked to the land.

However, farming went through many changes. Larger farms and plantations were set up and farming was geared to producing single crops, or cash crops, for export. These included coffee, cocoa beans, and timber, all of which were exported to bring in foreign currency. Again, focusing only on crops for export meant that subsistence farmers began to lose land as it was cleared for more intensive methods. Intensive farming also overworked the land, leaving the soil vulnerable to damage and erosion. Traditionally, Africans had used slash-and-burn methods to clear land in the rainforests, but, as more trees were cleared and the rainforest was exploited to obtain timber to earn foreign currency, deforestation became an increasing problem.

Urbanization
Population growth was rapid during the 1980s. As

population grew, so too did the development of towns and cities. After independence, and as more urban-based jobs were created, increasing numbers of people moved from the country to towns and cities in search of work. Capital cities, ports, and mining towns exerted the strongest pull. By the early 1990s, Zambia was one of Africa's most urbanized countries, with many third- and fourth-generation town dwellers living in the Copperbelt.

The rapid growth of numbers in towns put huge pressures on services, such as housing, water, electricity, and sanitation, which could not always cope with the inflow of people. Disease and epidemics were common, and shanty towns sprang up next to new skyscrapers. Jobs were not always available, leading to some unemployment and crime. Urbanization also took resources away from the countryside and put pressure on rural areas to provide more food for the growing urban populations.

Toward the new millennium

By the early 1990s, the economic picture in Central Africa was varied. In most countries, dictatorships and single-party systems were giving way to multiparty democracies and rich mineral resources offered hope of development.

However, conflict continued in Angola and the Democratic Republic of Congo, damaging the economic development of what should have been rich countries. Famine and drought were also appearing, while a growing number of refugees, fleeing conflicts in the region, were becoming an increasingly major problem.

Harvesting cocoa

The occupations of up to 80 percent of the population in Central Africa still remain closely linked to the land. Rather than subsistence farming, larger farms and plantations were set up. They were geared to single crops or cash crops for export, such as cocoa, which are exported to bring in foreign currency. Cash crops, however, are dependent on international prices; if these fail, then local economies suffer.

© DIAGRAM

Zambia since independence

Election results
Posters record the victory of Kenneth Kaunda in Northern Rhodesia in 1964. The country was renamed Zambia.

In 1964 the white-minority ruled colony of Northern Rhodesia achieved independence as Zambia. Free elections took place, based on universal suffrage, and Kenneth Kaunda, leader of the United National Independence Party (UNIP) became president. The government, like many others in Central Africa, faced serious problems left over from the colonial era. These included mounting ethnic rivalries, economic problems, clashes with white-dominated Southern Rhodesia, and a shortage of skilled and educated people – there were fewer than 100 African Zambian graduates in the country.

The Zambian economy was based on copper mining. Kaunda, who introduced socialist policies, proposed to use money from this to fund social programs, including free education and health. He also set out to reduce European economic influence. In 1969 the government took over most of the major firms, especially mining and banking companies. However, copper prices fell and the economy began to collapse. Kaunda's socialist policies actively discouraged foreign investment, but the large government-owned companies (parastatals) were inefficient and corrupt. In 1972 economic problems caused a split in UNIP, and Kaunda made Zambia a one-party state.

In 1965 Zambia, together with Britain and other countries, applied economic sanctions against white-ruled Rhodesia. In 1973 Rhodesia (now Zimbabwe) refused to allow Zambia to ship goods through its territory, so Tanzania, with Chinese help, built a new railroad from Dar es Salaam, which gave Zambia a trade route through friendly territory. A petroleum pipeline between Dar es Salaam and Ndola had been opened in 1968.

During the 1970s, economic sanctions against Rhodesia, and a drop in copper prices, put Zambia's economy under severe strain. In the 1980s, in order to obtain foreign aid, Kaunda was forced to introduce austerity measures. Shortage of basic goods, cuts in food subsidies and rising unemployment led to rioting and strikes, and demands for a return to a democratic system.

Democracy was restored in 1991 and Frederick Chiluba, a trade unionist and leader of the Movement for Multiparty Democracy (MMD), was elected president. He introduced economic reforms, including plans to privatize the copper industry, which eased economic conditions a little. But Zambia continued to be burdened by a huge international debt. By the late 1990s, the standard of living in Zambia was half what it had been in the mid-1960s. Unemployment and inflation were high and HIV/AIDS was becoming a major healthcare problem.

Hydroelectric power
The Kariba Dam was built in the 1950s at a cost of many millions of dollars, and also forced the relocation of numerous Zambian citizens.

Tanzam railway
The main trade route by which copper and other products are moved to ports for export is this railway. It links Zambia to the port of Dar es Salaam in neighboring Tanzania.

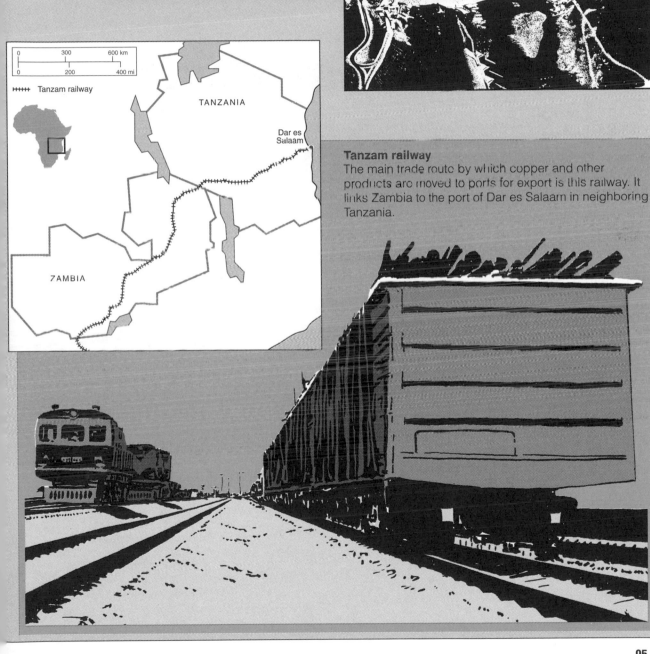

Debt in Central Africa

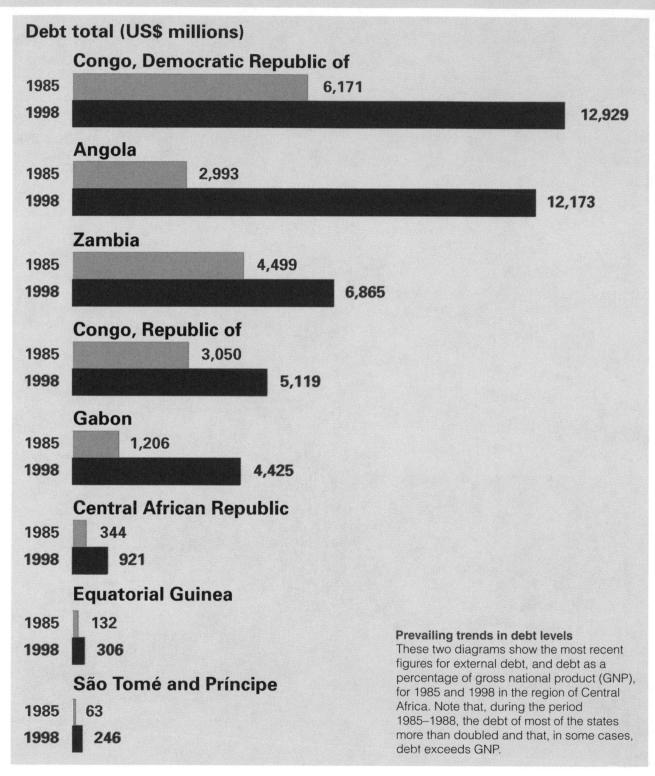

Debt total (US$ millions)

Congo, Democratic Republic of
1985 — 6,171
1998 — 12,929

Angola
1985 — 2,993
1998 — 12,173

Zambia
1985 — 4,499
1998 — 6,865

Congo, Republic of
1985 — 3,050
1998 — 5,119

Gabon
1985 — 1,206
1998 — 4,425

Central African Republic
1985 — 344
1998 — 921

Equatorial Guinea
1985 — 132
1998 — 306

São Tomé and Príncipe
1985 — 63
1998 — 246

Prevailing trends in debt levels
These two diagrams show the most recent figures for external debt, and debt as a percentage of gross national product (GNP), for 1985 and 1998 in the region of Central Africa. Note that, during the period 1985–1988, the debt of most of the states more than doubled and that, in some cases, debt exceeds GNP.

Debt as percentage of GNP (US$)

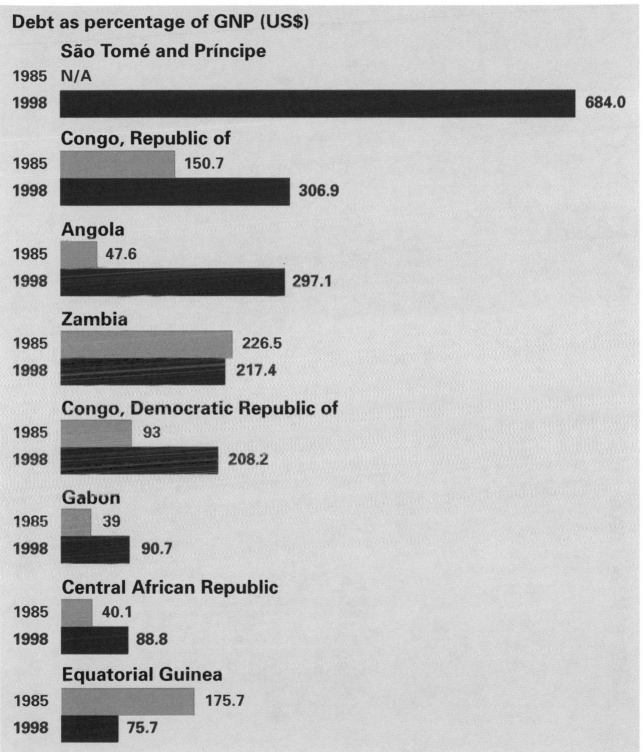

São Tomé and Príncipe
1985 N/A
1998 684.0

Congo, Republic of
1985 150.7
1998 306.9

Angola
1985 47.6
1998 297.1

Zambia
1985 226.5
1998 217.4

Congo, Democratic Republic of
1985 93
1998 208.2

Gabon
1985 39
1998 90.7

Central African Republic
1985 40.1
1998 88.8

Equatorial Guinea
1985 175.7
1998 75.7

© DIAGRAM

CENTRAL AFRICA TODAY

Prosperity
These diagrams show the gross national income (GNI) of the Central African states (below) as compared with that of the US (below right) in 2002. GNI is the official measure of the size of the individual economies in the region.

per capita Gross National Income in US$

$ = US$1,000

Gabon
$ $ $
3,190

Equatorial Guinea
$
700

Congo, Republic of
$
630

Zambia
$
300

São Tomé and Príncipe
$
290

Central African Republic
$
290

Angola
$
290

Congo, Democratic Republic of
N/A

Since independence, the countries of Central Africa have experienced many problems which have prevented them from achieving their full potential. Political instability, brutal dictatorships, and years of war and conflict have caused the deaths of millions, as well as damaging the social structures and economies of individual countries. War has, in turn, created refugee problems, and frequently devastating food crises.

Social poverty
Exploitation of natural resources, such as oil, uranium, and iron ore, has been a feature of Central Africa since independence. The revenues produced should have brought wealth to the region, but corrupt governments and the drive to finance continuing conflict have left Central African countries among the poorest in the world.

In Angola, where fertile land and abundant resources should make it a wealthy country, continual war has resulted in an average annual income of only $290, compared with an average annual income of $34,100 in the United States. In the Democratic Republic of Congo, also torn by war, the average annual income drops to $110. Only in Gabon, the wealthiest country in the region, does average annual income rise to $3,190.

Life expectancy in most of the region is also low, ranging between 38 years in Zambia to 52 years in Gabon, compared with a life expectancy of 77 years in the US. Only in São Tomé and Príncipe is life expectancy as high as 65.

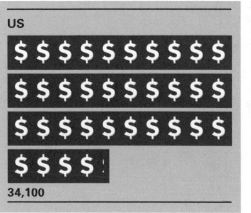

US
$ $ $ $ $ $ $ $ $
$ $ $ $ $ $ $ $ $
$ $ $ $ $ $ $ $ $
$ $ $ $
34,100

Factors causing poverty in Africa
- Political corruption
- Civil war
- Racial conflict
- Low technical skills in the workforce
- Ownership of local industry in "Western" hands
- Profits remaining outside African continent
- Uncontrollable diseases

Uranium (left)
The successful exploitation of natural resources, such as uranium, has been a feature of Central Africa since it became independent. This uranium factory is situated at Mounana in Gabon, a country which currently boasts one of the most successful economies in the entire continent of Africa.

The *Zafiro Producer* (below)
Traditionally, oil fields have been produced by building a platform on the site. On smaller oil fields, where it is not economically viable to build a platform, a cheaper option, called a Floating Production Storage and Offloading (FPSO) vessel, is now used. This one, originally an oil tanker, was converted into an FPSO and sent to Bioko Island, off the coast of Equatorial Guinea, in 1997.

Economic success

Gabon is the most economically successful country in the region. Its exploitation of petroleum, natural gas, uranium and metal ores has made it one of the most successful economies in Africa.

By the early 1990s, the economy of Equatorial Guinea was also growing fast, stimulated by oil revenue.

Zambia, now almost free of ethnic conflict and the most stable country in Central Africa, is the world's fourth largest producer of copper.

The struggle for democracy

Leading by right
Pascal Lissouba (left) became president of the Republic of Congo in the first free elections since democracy was restored to the country in 1992. Teodoro Obiang Nguema Mbsango (right) was reelected as president of Equatorial Guinea in 1996 and 2002, despite accusations of fraud.

Some Central African countries experienced brutal dictatorships. In the Democratic Republic of the Congo, President Mobutu ruled as a corrupt dictator for more than 30 years before being overthrown. Brutal despots ruled the Central African Republic and Equatorial Guinea for many years. In Equatorial Guinea, thousands were executed or fled into exile purged by the harsh regime of Francisco Macías Nguema, which lasted from 1970 until he was finally overthrown and executed in 1979.

Since the early 1990s, however, multiparty constitutions and democratic institutions have been restored to Central Africa. Free elections are a feature of the region today, even though charges of electoral corruption and fraud still occur. One of the major challenges facing Central Africa today is to develop democratic institutions that truly meet the needs of the people.

Fragile peace
Since Angola became independent in 1975, it has undergone more than 30 years of almost continuous civil war, mainly between the government, backed by communist powers, and the Union for the Total

Political instability in Central Africa: 1990–2002

Angola	Central African Republic	Congo, Dem. Rep. of
1990 MPLA renounces Marxism	**1992** Multiparty constitution introduced	**1990** Mobutu lifts ban on political parties
1991 MPLA and UNITA agree a ceasefire	**1993** Ange-Félix Patassé becomes president after multiparty elections	**1991** Economic problems lead to rioting
1992 MPLA's José Eduardo dos Santos becomes president after multiparty elections. UNITA begins the civil war again	**1996** France helps to suppress military rebellion	**1994** One million Hutu refugees flee to Zaïre from Rwanda
1994 New peace agreement signed by MPLA and UNITA	**1997** President Patassé calls for the withdrawal of French troops amid growing anti-French hostility	**1995** Outbreak of Ebola virus in Kikwit
1995 UN peacekeeping force oversees peace agreement	**1998** UN force arrives in CAR to replace French troops	**1996** Hutu-Tutsi conflict in Rwanda and Burundi spreads to the Tutsi of eastern Zaïre
1997 New government of national unity formed	**1999** Patassé is reelected president, defeating Kolingba	**1997** Laurent Kabila overthrows Mobutu government and becomes president with support of Tutsi forces: name changed to Democratic Republic of Congo
1999 Civil war breaks out again between MPLA and UNITA	**2001** Attempted coup is put down with Libyan help	**1998** Civil war breaks out. Angola, Chad, Namibia and Zimbabwe send forces to support Kabila against rebels supported by Burundi, Rwanda and Uganda
2000 UNITA launches new offensives, continuing the civil war	**2002** President Patassé meets President Déby of Chad to discuss tensions between the two countries. In October, CAR accuses Chad of supporting a failed rebellion	**2001** Kabila is assassinated; succeeded by his son, Major-General Joseph Kabila
2002 Jonas Savimbi is killed in action and a ceasefire is agreed		**2002** Peace talks fail to end civil conflict

Independence of Angola (UNITA), which was backed by South Africa and Western powers. Finally, in April 2002, UNITA agreed to a ceasefire and a peace deal was achieved. The cost to the country has been enormous. Thousands have died and an estimated 4 million displaced. By July 2002, the signs were that war was subsiding, but Angola was facing a huge food and refugee crisis, which was made worse by drought.

The Democratic Republic of Congo also experienced years of civil war, made worse from 1996 when the ethnic Hutu and Tutsi conflict spilled over into the eastern part of the country. In July 2002, Rwanda and the Democratic Republic of Congo finally agreed to end the conflict, which had claimed millions of civilian lives. According to the United Nations some 2 million civilians had died from starvation and disease. The country's economy and society had been left in turmoil. Its mineral wealth had been looted and there was a massive refugee problem.

In 2002 Angola and the Democratic Republic of Congo were facing a crisis. The UN estimated that, in the Congo, some 16 million people were starving. Observers hoped that peace would hold.

Leading by might
Jonas Malheiro Savimbi (left) set up UNITA to oppose Portuguese rule in Angola in 1966. After independence in 1975 he continued to lead UNITA in a guerrilla war against the government. Laurent Desiré Kabila (right) became president of Democratic Republic of Congo in 1997 following a rebellion against the regime led by Mobutu Sese Seko.

Congo, Republic of

1990 Marxism renounced

1991 Political parties legalized

1992 Multiparty constitution approved by a referendum: country resumes name of Republic of Congo

1993 President Sassou-Nguesso defeated in elections by Pascal Lissouba

1997 Sassou-Nguesso seizes power supported by Angolans

1998 Republic of Congo and Democratic Republic of Congo negotiate common frontier

1999 Fighting concluded

2002 Sassou-Nguesso wins first elections since 1992

Equatorial Guinea

1992 Multiparty constitution introduced

1993 Democratic Party wins 68 of 80 seats in elections

1996 Obiang Nguema re-elected as president amid allegations of vote rigging

1998 Arrests of Bubi separatists on Bioko Island

1999 National elections won by ruling Democratic Party amid accusations of fraud

2001 Economy grows quickly as a result of oil exploitation

2002 Equatorial Guinea and Nigeria sign agreement over utilization of offshore oil on their maritime boundaries. Obiang Nguema is reelected president

Gabon

1990 Opposition parties legalized: ruling Gabonese Democratic party wins assembly elections

1993 Bongo retains the presidency after winning first multiparty elections

1996 Gabon withdraws from OPEC

1998 Bongo wins presidential elections with 66 percent of vote

2001 Gabonese Democratic Party wins overwhelming victory in legislative elections

2002 Outbreak of the deadly Ebola virus causes alarm

Zambia

1990 Opposition parties legalized

1991 Frederick Chiluba of Movement for Multiparty Democracy (MMD) defeats Kaunda in first multiparty elections

1993 State of emergency declared to undermine campaign of civil disobedience by supporters of UNIP

1996 Chiluba reelected president

1997 Kaunda barred from standing for election after failed coup

2001 MMD candidate Levy Mwanawasa elected president

© DIAGRAM

Refugees

Civil war, ethnic conflict, and religious or political persecution have created a refugee crisis in Central Africa. Some refugees have fled from conflicts or persecution within the region itself; others have come to Central Africa from conflicts or persecution elsewhere.

By the end of 2001, more than 1 million people from the Central African region were refugees, and a further 3 million were displaced within their own countries. While African nations are normally generous to refugees, their very presence puts a strain on already overburdened services.

Children as victims (above)
Conflict between the Hutu government and Tutsi rebels in Rwanda in 1994 erupted into violence, with the result that hundreds of thousands of people, many of whom were children, were forced to escape from the fighting.

Cause for concern (below)
This diagram shows the number of refugees and asylum-seekers, delineated according to eventual country of asylum, at the end of 2001.

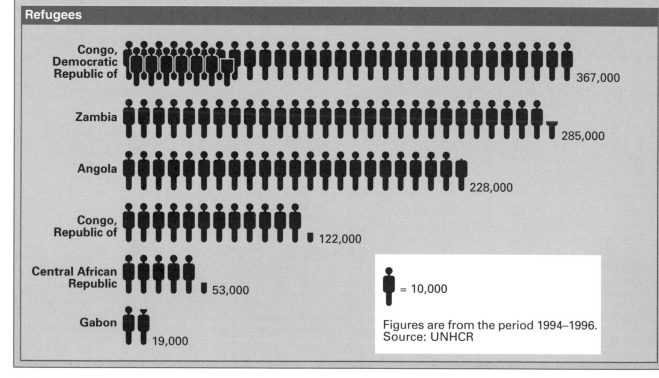

Refugees

Congo, Democratic Republic of	367,000
Zambia	285,000
Angola	228,000
Congo, Republic of	122,000
Central African Republic	53,000
Gabon	19,000

= 10,000

Figures are from the period 1994–1996.
Source: UNHCR

Angola

This nation is host to refugees from the Democratic Republic of Congo, Rwanda, and Burundi. During Angola's bitter civil war, many Angolans fled the country to find refuge in countries, such as the Democratic Republic of Congo, Zambia, and Namibia. As yet, few Angolans have returned, many being deterred by conditions within the country, and the presence of at least 1 million landmines.

Democratic Republic of Congo

In 2001, there were about 367,000 refugees in the Democratic Republic of Congo, and more than 2 million displaced persons. The country is host to many refugees from neighboring countries.

During the mid-1990s, more than 2 million Rwandans arrived seeking asylum. The country began to repatriate them in 1995, but there was an international outcry and the United Nations High Commission for Refugees (UNHCR) took over the task. Thousands more arrived from Rwanda and Burundi in 1996, triggering civil war in the Demcratic Republic of Congo (formerly Zaïre.) Other refugees in the region include Ugandans, avoiding political persecution, and Angolans, fleeing civil war.

Local people have also fled out of the country as refugees, particularly those escaping Mobutu's dictatorship. Angola, Burundi, South Africa, Tanzania, and Uganda all contain refugees from the Democratic Republic of Congo.

Zambia

Compared with other countries in the region, Zambia enjoys stability, and is a popular destination for refugees. In 2001 it sheltered refugees from the Democratic Republic of Congo, Rwanda, and Burundi.

Equatorial Guinea

One of the largest movements of refugees out of a Central African country took place during the 1970s, when an estimated third of the population fled Macias Nguema's dictatorship. They included some of the most skilled of the country's people.

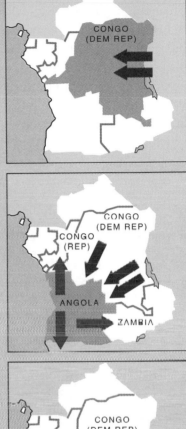

Movement of refugees (right)
These four maps show the direction from which numerous refugees recently entered the Central African nation states of Angola, Democratic Republic of Congo, and Zambia.

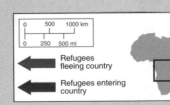

Refugees fleeing country

Refugees entering country

© DIAGRAM

Coups d'État in Central Africa

Independence from colonial rule by various European powers proved difficult to achieve for many African nations. Yet, once the battle for independence had been won, a variety of problems beset the new states.

As the maps (right) show, some nations were subject to political instability and military *coups d'état* after independence.

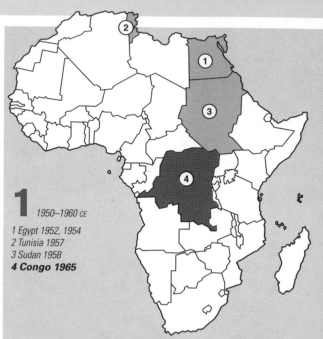

1 1950–1960 CE

1 Egypt 1952, 1954
2 Tunisia 1957
3 Sudan 1958
4 Congo 1965

The "emperor" of the Central African Empire
Jean Bédel Bokassa, the former commander of the army of the Central African Republic, seized power in 1966 and served as president until 1976, when he declared himself "emperor" of the Central African Empire. Overthrown in 1979, he went into exile but returned in 1986, only to serve six years in prison.

Coups d'état in Central Africa
Some presidents who recently held office in Central Africa.

Laurent Kabila
President of the Democratic Republic of Congo from 1997, he was assassinated in 2001.

David Dacko
He became the first president of the Central African Republic in 1960.

Marien Ngouabi
President of the Republic of Congo from 1970, he was assassinated in 1977.

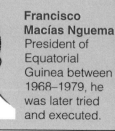

André Kolingba
He seized power from David Dacko in the CAR in a peaceful coup in 1981.

Francisco Macías Nguema
President of Equatorial Guinea between 1968–1979, he was later tried and executed.

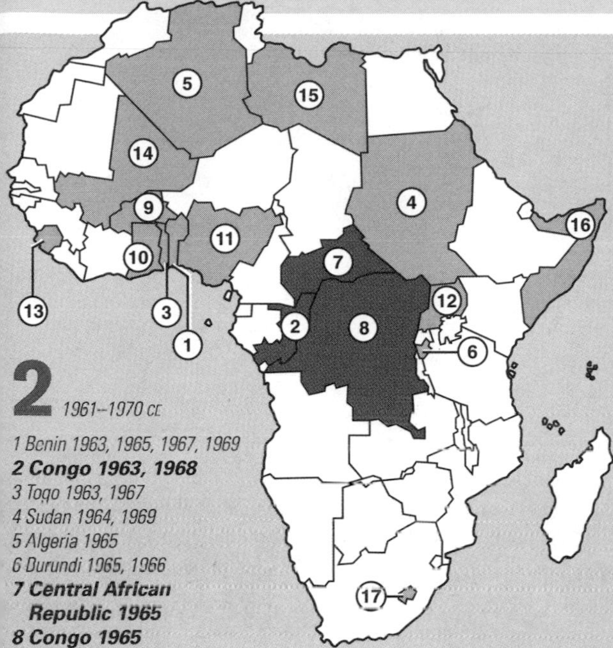

2 1961–1970 CE

1 Benin 1963, 1965, 1967, 1969
2 Congo 1963, 1968
3 Togo 1963, 1967
4 Sudan 1964, 1969
5 Algeria 1965
6 Burundi 1965, 1966
**7 Central African
Republic 1965**
8 Congo 1965
9 Burkina Faso 1966
10 Ghana 1966
11 Nigeria 1966
12 Uganda 1966
13 Sierra Leone 1967, 1968

14 Mali 1968
15 Libya 1969
16 Somalia 1969
17 Lesotho 1970

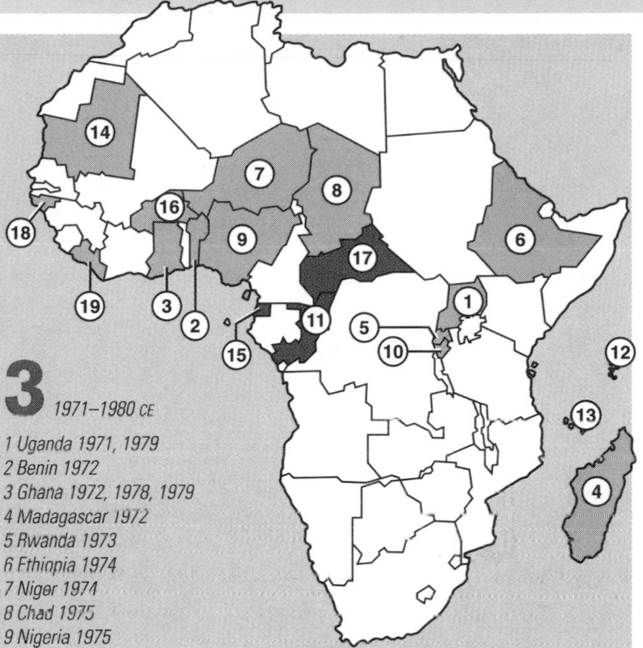

3 1971–1980 CE

1 Uganda 1971, 1979
2 Benin 1972
3 Ghana 1972, 1978, 1979
4 Madagascar 1972
5 Rwanda 1973
6 Ethiopia 1974
7 Niger 1974
8 Chad 1975
9 Nigeria 1975
10 Burundi 1976
11 Congo 1977
12 Seychelles 1977
13 Comoros 1978
14 Mauritania 1978, 1980

15 Equatorial Guinea 1979
16 Burkina Faso 1980
17 Central African Republic 1980
18 Guinea-Bissau 1980
19 Liberia 1900

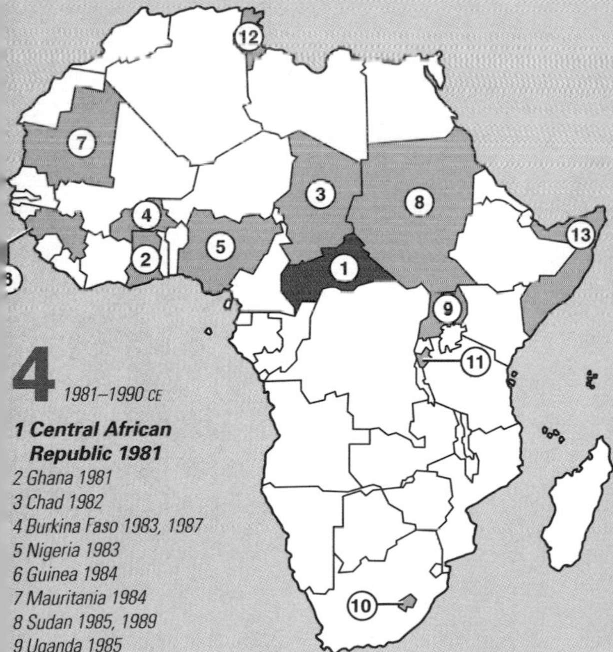

4 1981–1990 CE

**1 Central African
Republic 1981**
2 Ghana 1981
3 Chad 1982
4 Burkina Faso 1983, 1987
5 Nigeria 1983
6 Guinea 1984
7 Mauritania 1984
8 Sudan 1985, 1989
9 Uganda 1985
10 Lesotho 1986
11 Burundi 1987
12 Tunisia 1987

13 Somalia 1990

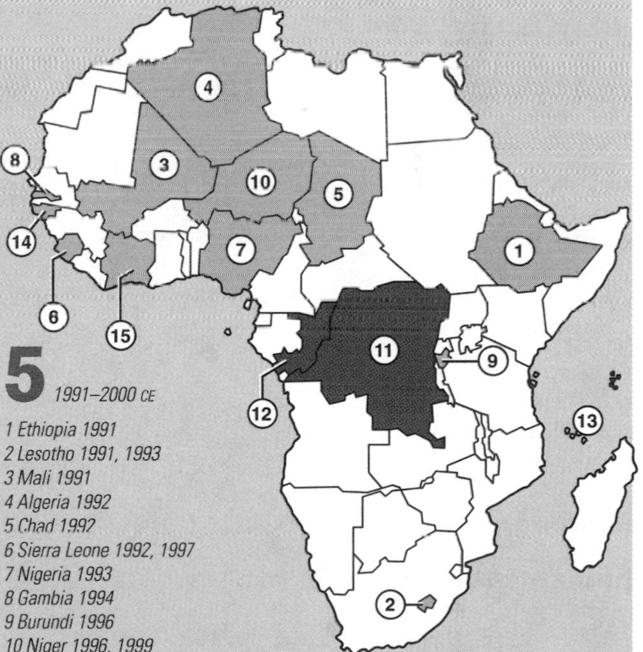

5 1991–2000 CE

1 Ethiopia 1991
2 Lesotho 1991, 1993
3 Mali 1991
4 Algeria 1992
5 Chad 1992
6 Sierra Leone 1992, 1997
7 Nigeria 1993
8 Gambia 1994
9 Burundi 1996
10 Niger 1996, 1999
11 Congo, Dem. Rep. 1997
**12 Congo, Republic of
1997**

13 Comoros 1999
14 Guinea-Bissau 1999
15 Ivory Coast 1999

© DIAGRAM

105

GLOSSARY

abolitionist A person who campaigned to abolish, or bring to an end, the slave trade and slavery. Abolitionists included both black and white campaigners.

Bantu Large group of related African languages. The word literally means "people." Most black Africans in Central Africa today are descended from Bantu-speaking peoples who settled the continent from about 100 CE.

BCE Before Common Era.

CE Common Era.

chiefdom A territory or area governed by a chief.

clan A group of people who claim descent from a common ancestor or ancestors.

Cold War Name given to the struggle for power between the former Soviet Union, and its allies, and the United States, and its allies. It lasted from 1946 until the collapse of Communism in 1991. The so-called superpowers did not actually fight each other, but often backed opposing sides in other parts of the world, engaging in proxy wars.

colony A country, region or territory occupied or settled by people from another country, and usually controlled by that country. The people who settle the colony are called colonists.

communism A political and economic philosophy based on the beliefs of Karl Marx. Communists believe that there should be no private property and that all land, factories and so on should be owned by the people.

coup A seizure of power, usually illegal. A military coup describes seizure of power by the army or other military forces.

deforestation The clearing or cutting down of trees in a forest.

democracy A system of government in which all adults take part in the process of governing by electing representatives.

erosion Wearing down of rocks or other substances. Soil erosion is caused by overuse of soil by farming or deforestation.

guerrilla Member of a independent group of fighters, rather than being part of a state's official armed forces.

hominid Member of the primate family Hominidae, including humans and their ancestors.

hunter-gatherers People who survive by hunting animals and gathering plants.

IMF The acronym used for the International Monetary Fund. It is an international organization which encourages international monetary cooperation, and also provides credit facilities to developing countries.

imperialism Either the policy, or the practice, of extending the rule of one state over other, formerly independent, territories.

infrastructure Basic structural systems or foundations on which a society is built, such as roads, services, sanitation, and so on.

humanitarian Someone who works for the good of people, and puts humans first.

matrilineal Descent through the mother.

nationalized When the state or government takes control and runs businesses or industries.

nationalist Someone who fights for his or her nation.

OPEC The acronym used for the Organization of Petroleum Exporting Countries.

pastoralists People who keep herds of animals, such as sheep, on land known as pasture.

protectorate A state that is controlled or protected by another nation or state. Similar to colony.

racism Discrimination against a person or group of persons on the ground of race; most commonly used to describe discrimination by white against black people.

refugee A person who flees from his or her home or country to escape from danger.

republic A country or state in which power is held by the people, or their elected government, or an elected or non-elected president.

"Scramble" for Africa Term used to describe how rival European powers raced to obtain colonies in Africa during the late 19th century.

slash-and-burn A type of cultivation used in forests. Trees are cut down and burned, clearing a patch of land which is used for a short time only.

subsistence farming A type of farming in which most or all of the crop is used by the farmer and farming family who work the land. The farmer is left with little or nothing to sell.

suffrage The right to vote in an election.

"Triangular trade" A term used to describe the route taken by slave traders which went, broadly speaking, in the shape of a triangle from Europe to Africa and then on to the Americas.

UN The acronym used for the United Nations.

urbanization Development of towns and cities. Urbanization may involve making a rural (country) area more urban, or may describe the movement of people from country into towns.

Bibliography

Africa South of the Sahara, London: Europa Publications (2001)

Beauclerk, J., *Hunters and Gatherers in Central Africa*, Oxford (UK): Oxfam (1994)

Birmingham, David, and Martin, Phyllis, *History of Central Africa*, New York: Longman (1983)

Brockman, N.C., *An African Biographical Dictionary*, Santa Barbara, CA.: ABC-Clio Longman (1994)

Carr-Hill, Roy, A., *Social Conditions in Sub-Saharan Africa*, Basingstoke (UK): Macmillan (1990)

Clark, J.D., *Cambridge History of Africa*, Cambridge (UK): Cambridge University Press (1982)

Diagram Group, *African History On File*, New York: Facts On File (2003)

Diagram Group, *Encyclopedia of African Nations*, New York: Facts On File (2002)

Diagram Group, *Encyclopedia of African Peoples*, New York: Facts On File (2000)

Diagram Group, *Peoples of Central Africa*, New York: Facts On File (1997)

Diagram Group, *Religions On File*, New York: Facts On File (1990)

Diagram Group, *Timelines On File*, 4 vols. New York: Facts On File (2000)

Fage, J.D., with Tordoff, William, *A History of Africa*, 4th ed. New York and London: Routledge (2002)

Glickman, Harvey, ed., *Political Leaders of Contemporary Africa South of the Sahara*, Westport, Conn.: Greenwood Press (1992)

Hay. Margaret Jean, and Stichter, Sharon, eds., *African Women South of the Sahara*, New York: Longman (1984)

Koloss, H. J., *Art of Central Africa*, New York: Metropolitan Museum of Art (1990)

Lipschutz, M., and Rasmussen, R., *Dictionary of African Historical Biography*, Oxford (UK): Heinemann (1978)

Mack, J., *Emil Torday and the Art of the Congo*, London: British Museum

Middleton, John, ed., *Encyclopedia of Africa: South of the Sahara*, 4 vols. New York: Scribner's (1997)

Middleton, John, and Rassam, A., *Encyclopedia of World Cultures: Africa and the Middle East*, Boston, MA.: G.K.Hall & Co. (1995)

Morrison, D., Mitchell, R., and Paden, J., *Black Africa: A Comparative Handbook*, New York: Innington Publishers Inc.(1984)

Moss, J., and Wilson, G., *Peoples of the World: Africans South of the Sahara*, Detroit, Ill.: Gale Research (1991)

Needham, D.E., Mashingaidze, E. K., and Bhebe, N., *From Iron Age to Independence. A History of Central Africa*, Harlow (UK): Longman Group (1984)

Rake, A., *100 Great Africans*, Metuchen, NJ.: Scarecrow Press (1994)

Sub-Saharan Africa: From Crisis to Sustainable Growth, Washington, D.C.: World Bank (1989)

Turnbull, C., *The Mbuti Pygmies: Change and Adaption*, New York: Holt, Rinehart & Winston (1983)

Index

Index

Index

poverty 98
Príncipe 6, 8, 25, 42, 52, 65–8, 75, 77, 87, 89
pygmies 18

R

rainfall in Central Africa 7
Redjambe, Joseph 85
refugees 93, 102–3, 107
religions of Central Africa 5
Rhodes, Cecil 62–3, 72
Rhodesia 63, 65, 71–3, 94
Roberto, Holden 75, 78
Rwanda 83, 100–2

S

Salazar, Antonio de Oliviera 67
São Tomé 6, 8, 25, 28, 42, 52, 65–8, 75, 77, 87, 89
Sassou-Nguesso, Denis 84–5, 101
Savimbi, Jonas 75, 100–1
Savimbi, Roberto 78–9
Schweinfurth, Georg August 54, 60
Schweitzer, Albert 54, 57
Shabunda 83
slavery and the slave trade 12, 25–43, 52–66, 107
abolition of 40–1

Smith, Adam 40
Société des Amies des Noirs 40
Songye people 44
Southwest Africa People's Organization (SWAPO) 78
Soviet Union 77–80
Spanish influence in Central Africa 36, 40–1, 52, 66, 68, 86–7
Spanish language 10
Stanley, Henry Morton 52–60
subsistence farming 92, 107

T

Tanzam railway 95
Teke people 68
temperatures in Central Africa 7
Tippu Tip 34, 41, 58, 68
trade and trading routes 12, 18–28 *passim*, 34–9, 42, 46–7, 50, 52, 68
Trans-Gabon railway 90–1
Trovoada, Miguel 75, 87
Tshombe, Moise 77, 80–1
tumbas 29
Tutsis 77, 81, 83, 100–2

U

UNITA (*União Nacional para a Independência Total de Angola*) 75–81, 100–1
United Nations
High Commission for Refugees 103
peacekeeping missions 75, 80–1, 84, 100
uranium 99
urbanization 92–3, 107
US 40, 77–8

V

Vienna, Congress of (1815) 60

W

Wilberforce, William 40

Y

Yamba, Dauti 65
Yhombi-Opango, Joachim 84–5
Youlou, Fulbert 84

Z

Zaïre 65, 76–7, 81–3, 89, 100–3
Zambia 8, 72–3, 76–7, 89, 93–4, 99–103
Zanzibar, Sultan of 41